4th
TIME'S
a
CHARM

13 Lessons and 39 Questions
to Transform Your
Marriage and Your Life

Danielle
HOPE WOLFE

DANIELLE HOPE WOLFE
4th Time's a Charm
13 Lessons and 39 Questions to Transform Your Marriage and Your Life

Published by Danielle Hope Wolfe
Copyright © 2019 by Danielle Hope Wolfe
First Edition

PAPERBACK ISBN 978-0-578-51443-7

COVER & BOOK DESIGN Jazmin Welch
EDITOR Lori Bamber
AUTHOR PORTRAIT PHOTOGRAPHY Shelby Miller Photography
PUBLISHING SUPPORT The Self Publishing Agency

To Jason, Austin, Kole, Cooper and Jackson.
You are my every reason for breathing, my heart and soul.
I will love you forever.

contents

PREFACE   1

LESSON 1   9
Learn to Love Yourself at Any Cost

LESSON 2   37
Marriage is a Partnership,
Not a Competition

LESSON 3   47
You Get to Choose Your
Perception of Your Life

LESSON 4   67
Both Partners Have to
be in the Marriage

LESSON 5   81
Grace Transforms
Mistakes into Wisdom

LESSON 6   89
You Know What's Best for the Kids? Love.

LESSON 7   107
Step-Parenting. It's Hard.

LESSON 8   117
You Can Fall in Love Again!

LESSON 9 133
Get on the Same Page Financially.
P.S. The Saver is Right!

LESSON 10 147
Choose to be Spiritual Partners

LESSON 11 157
The Ripple Effect

LESSON 12 171
Loyalty is Earned Through Action

LESSON 13 179
Learn How to Communicate
With Each Other

IN CLOSING 199

RESOURCES 207

preface

When I first decided to write a book, my plan was to write only about marriage—what worked, what failed, and what blew up in my face.

Throughout the book's evolution, however, I've realized it's impossible to talk about a loving marriage without talking about self-love and its opposite, shame.

I've lived a great deal of my life in shame because I have a history of failed marriages. Three, in fact, by the age of 26.

Yikes, am I right??

I am sure you can imagine the looks on the faces of my family when I told them I was getting hitched just one more time at the age of 27. (I promised them it would be my last attempt.) And despite making me the punchline for jokes about a record number of weddings, marrying Jason was the best decision of my life.

The intention I've set for this book is to stand in truth and vulnerability and share my stories, along with what I've learned along the way. There have been so many teachers whose beautiful work spoke to me and changed my perceptions of relationships. I'm now passing it all on—it is my hope that you'll find these pages useful in creating your own joyous life.

While writing, I have continued to grow spiritually, something I'm committed to doing throughout my life. At 19, expecting my first son and attempting to fill the roles of adult, wife, mother, student and professional, I was so naive. I had no idea that I had to grow emotionally and stop projecting all my fears of inadequacy onto other people. Getting real and honest with myself was a process that took several decades.

I walked around in a sort of half-sleep, not thinking about growing spiritually or emotionally—not knowing, to paraphrase the meme, that I had to be the change I wanted to see in my life. It wasn't until my brother Mike was killed in a motorcycle accident and I was diagnosed with multiple sclerosis a few years later that I began opening to the possibilities of a new path.

I had lost sight of the things that mattered most to me in the world. I wanted so much for everybody to believe that I was successful—my parents, family, friends, peers, the preschool moms, the working moms—everybody, including people I'd never met and people whose values I didn't share.

I'd lost myself, or perhaps never found myself, morphing to fit in anywhere I could. The way I lived my life in those years didn't honor or serve my true self, but it eventually taught me that I needed to heal the wounds of my past—that it was my responsibility to do so. Life knocked me to my knees. It made me reevaluate my path and myself in a way that gave me no choice but to face my deepest wounds.

Accepting my own darkness was the most difficult part of this process for me. But I began working on my inner wounds and learning to let go and forgive. I began to awaken. I had crazy paranormal occurrences for months after my brother's death, which lead me down a path of mediumship, a way of orienting my consciousness to the most subtle of messages from others in this life and beyond. As I took courses and learned the practices, I began the painstaking process of peeling back my trauma, grief and ineffective coping mechanisms, layer by layer.

I had to shed the roles I'd put on to cover my insecurities and discover who I truly am: what I love to do, who I love to work with, where I feel drawn to focus my attention and energy, and what feeds my soul. Doing so has given me the ability to love my husband and children at a much deeper and more compassionate level.

I loved my nursing career. But after losing my big brother to a motorcycle accident, I began having difficulty with my feelings toward patients and their families. I was so emotionally connected to their suffering that I was unable to set my feelings aside. Compartmentalizing is a necessary coping mechanism for healthcare professionals, and when I lost that ability, it was difficult to make quick decisions in the high-stress intensive care unit where I worked. The stress became too much. Each time I stepped onto the floor at work, I relived Mike's accident and the trauma of taking him off life support and saying goodbye.

In addition to trying to manage these emotional triggers, I was slowly beginning to see that I expected Jason to fill the void of belonging and acceptance that I'd missed growing up. Somewhere deep down inside, I had expected each of my husbands to save me—to make me happy and fulfill my deep unmet need to feel safe, loved and accepted.

Learning mediumship was and continues to be a hugely powerful process in my spiritual growth. It led me to self-discovery and equipped me with coping techniques that have helped me grow emotionally, grieve for my brother and manage my health limitations. It's helped me grow from an emotional toddler into a mature human being.

Growth for me is the daily, conscious effort to be a person who isn't overtaken by every emotional reaction.

Along the way, I have come to understand that we must accept ourselves just as we are, with all our imperfections, free of judgment, to have beautiful relationships of any kind. We must fall head over heels, madly, deeply, unconditionally in love with ourselves. This kind of love doesn't come from ego, but from inner compassion. Our ego wants us to believe that we are either better or worse than other people; self-love tells us that we are the most special person in the universe and everyone else is too. Self-love allows us to sit comfortably in that quiet, empty space deep down in the middle of our chests, the place where we feel all of life's biggest emotions.

You will notice this theme throughout this book—I talk a lot about the need to look inside and learn to love ourselves. Without self-love, our egos will never step back to allow our higher selves to steer us in the direction of our own joy.

My spiritual journey has been a huge wakeup call. It taught me that loving myself is the life force of a joyous life and marriage. Learning to stand in my power and vulnerability, sharing my lowest of lows and highest of highs, has healed me and my marriage on levels too few people get to experience.

I feel so blessed. Reflection has taught me so much about where I started and why, who I became through painful experience, and how I learned to unravel the destructive emotions and unhealthy coping mechanisms of my past.

I had to do this inner work in order to release the expectation I had placed on my husband to bring me happiness. I learned there was only one person on the planet who could find the joy waiting within—me! It was time to take on that responsibility.

Transformational speaker Lisa Nichols talks about loving yourself and honoring your story. I came across her famous Steve Harvey interview on Facebook. If you haven't had a chance to watch it, I encourage you to google it. She is so raw and pure, living her power and refusing to be defined by her past circumstances. She embraces her story and uses it to uplift others, provide hope and inspire the world. Watching Lisa, I felt called to share my experiences with you.

Yes, I'm on marriage number four. And every step on that path left me with valuable lessons about what does and doesn't work. Together, Jason and I have built a beautiful marriage, friendship, spiritual partnership and covenant. I want to share the powerful tools I've been given on this journey, the lessons that transformed our sometimes-rocky relationship into a rock-solid marriage.

Jason and I have had very low moments. We have endured the loss of parents, siblings, moves across state lines, struggles and triumphs. We even considered divorce early in our marriage. I'm grateful every day that we didn't give up on each other.

During some of our most difficult times, we were able to recognize that our relationship wasn't working. But neither were we willing to give up on it. We were both committed to looking in the mirror, recognizing our own personal darkness. We evaluated the ways we were acting, treating each other and living. We recognized that if we continued down the path we were walking, it would eventually mean the end of our life together. Then we acted on that understanding, changing our behaviors. We started working together at growing and loving, and at putting our marriage first.

We found that if we are willing to stop projecting our own insecurities and blaming each other long enough to see our current path isn't going to end well, it gives us the power to map a new direction.

Jason and I have put in the time and effort to regain love, respect and admiration for ourselves and each other. With each struggle we face in life and love, we gain more valuable tools and lessons.

I understand fully that there is no "one size fits all" in marriage, but I believe these tools can be adapted to solve whatever challenges you face.

Every experience, good and bad, is an opportunity to learn. Within these pages, you will find the evolution of our relationship, the sources that helped it evolve to where it is today, and the tools we use to continue growing to the next levels—while experiencing so much joy in our journey together.

To protect the privacy of my ex-husbands, I refer to them as ex-husbands number one, two and three, in chronological order.

the lessons

When I first considered putting pen to paper and creating this book, I had an internal dialogue along the lines of, "Why in the world would someone who has been married four times write a book about creating a strong and joyous marriage?" Or, "What could I possibly know that could help other people with their relationships?"

I hadn't quite come to terms with the unparalleled power of making mistakes and learning from them. But sitting here right now, typing away on my keyboard at the age of 39, I can confidently say I have some amazing stuff to share.

➤ **AN IMPORTANT NOTE BEFORE WE GET STARTED:** None of this applies to you right now if you are currently in an abusive relationship. If you or your children are being abused, you need to focus on getting to safety. And never forget that emotional abuse is just as damaging as physical abuse, sometimes even more so. Please see the resources in the back of the book and reach out for help.

Through a lot of trial and error and by reading many self-help books and going to therapy, Jason and I began looking inward on a regular basis. We began to be accountable to ourselves and each other. We had the desire to improve our relationship through love, respect, humility and, most of all, grace and forgiveness. I know these practices can serve you too.

LEARN TO LOVE YOURSELF AT ANY COST

Most of my life, I hated pretty much everything about Danielle.

At 19 years old, four months pregnant, I allowed the opinions of others to rule my life and decisions. My first husband and I didn't want to get married. He never even proposed. We had a typical shotgun wedding.

We were babies having a baby, allowing our parents to make very serious decisions for us, while not fully considering or understanding how our actions would affect our child.

I was so disrespectful to my first husband and his feelings. I was hard and cold. I was a stonewaller, as described by relationship expert John Gottman—when my husband tried to talk things through with me, I withdrew. (If this sounds familiar to you, you'll find a lot more information on stonewalling in the fight, flight or freeze response sections coming up.)

As much as we wanted to, neither of us was mature enough to fulfill the roles we were trying to play to please our parents. We got through the wedding, but without happily coupled role models in our lives, we had no idea how to have a marriage.

Two years in, when my high school crush reached out to reconnect, I loved the attention. I felt like he would save me from the mess I'd created—it was a chance for a new start. I quickly and very disrespectfully ended my first marriage and jumped right into my second.

I didn't love myself, so I desperately wanted other people to give me their time, attention and love. My work and personal relationships suffered, and drama lurked around every corner. I loaded up the shame and hid it behind a "me against the world" attitude. Fear of not being or having enough grew to a truck-sized mass of anger and self-loathing, emotional baggage that I carried for the greater part of a decade.

Husband number two had suffered so much as a child in a troubled home. His primary coping mechanism was emotional manipulation. He once told me that his best and worst quality was his ability to spot deep insecurities in others and use them to his advantage. He saw mine from a mile away: my lack of self-worth.

Although I was never comfortable with my body, it hurt extra deep the first time he body-shamed me. Several months into our relationship, he brought me a beautifully wrapped gift on one of his weekend trips home from college. I carefully opened it and pulled out a pair of expensive jeans. I was thrilled. But as I unfolded them, I realized they looked like they were made to fit a child.

My heart sank. I sucked back the tears and tried to hide my feelings with a smile. My mind raced, confused and frustrated.

With a big smile, he said, "These are your goal jeans. I know that, with hard work, you can fit into these."

Being so insecure and unsure of who I was as a person, I gave away my power easily. His "gift" catapulted me into a rabbit hole of self-loathing and hatred. There I found food addiction, anorexia and bulimia, insatiable exercising, pill popping and yo-yo dieting. I tormented myself emotionally for the next decade.

What's the point of my story? The point is, because I didn't feel I was worthy, he had the power to make me feel I wasn't worthy. I hated who I had become. I hated myself for getting pregnant right out of high school, for having a failed marriage by the age of 21 and for losing many friends and family members because of my immature, energy-sucking ways.

In this fragile emotional state, I thought that if I put on a strong front and made sure everyone knew we were doing great financially, nobody could call me a failure.

The truth? I was failing. I was failing myself and my children. I was too afraid to take off my masks and love myself. I kept trying to be someone I wasn't, pushing myself further and further away from the beautiful life it was within my power to create. I felt alone. I didn't feel I had anyone in my life who loved me unconditionally. Because I judged myself and others so harshly, I felt only judgment from other people.

I couldn't see a way out. In the mindset I was in, everything was someone else's fault. Unless they changed their behavior, I was trapped. It was easy for me to feel that my negative feelings were justified, and my negative feelings regularly triggered destructive behavior.

My dad didn't love me enough ...

My mom didn't pay attention to me ...

My friend was rude ...

My spouse hurt me ...

They ...

Them ...

Pointing my finger. Projecting.

THE HEALING POWER OF OWNING YOUR EXPERIENCE

Whether you believe in the law of attraction or not, it's easy to see why this way of thinking attracts only others who think and act the same way. We've probably all heard the phrase "Show me your friends and I'll show you your future."

While I had a few beautiful and true friends, I had surrounded myself mostly with people who didn't respect themselves and their marriages. They were miserable, just like me. I attracted people who were negative and judgmental and talked badly about every person they came across. They were my fellow victims. We bitched and complained about our lives and coworkers and judged others every chance we got.

We considered it therapy. Good to get it all out, right? WRONG!!! Terrible, actually. It's completely disrespectful. And why on earth were we enveloping ourselves in such toxic energy?

From time to time, we all feel the need to vent or get a situation "off our chest." We're human. I still have the impulse to call and bitch to my girlfriends when I get pissed off about something.

Sometimes, when we're having a difficult time managing our feelings, it is helpful to share them with a wise person who will help us gain perspective. Processing is different than venting. It's easy to tell the difference: just imagine telling someone about a situation that recently happened that really upset you.

Think about how you would feel if that person said, "What is within your power to change that would make this situation better?" If that question upsets you even more—if the only response that would be okay is something along the lines of, "What a jerk! I wouldn't put up with that"—you're venting. No judgment. I've been there and will be again. But if we need to vent regularly, it's an indication we are giving away far too much of our energy and power.

Emotional freedom is about getting to a place within yourself where you don't need to vent or explode. It is possible to find healthier coping mechanisms, behaviors that move you toward happiness rather than keeping you stuck and hurting.

When we're upset, something within our subconscious is alerting us to danger. Our amygdala (the part of the brain that's sometimes called the lizard brain, because it evolved before mammals) goes into warp drive. Our body is flooded with adrenaline and cortisol; we're now in some degree of fight, flight or freeze mode. If the reaction is intense enough, we go into pure survival mode and stop thinking logically. We stop making decisions with our longer-term best interests in mind. We may feel the desire to start swinging, physically or verbally, or to run and hide. Some of us shut down and, as soon as possible, withdraw.

These are natural, hardwired reactions that have helped keep us alive for as long as humans have existed. Here's the problem, though: a threat to our sense of self can feel as dangerous as a threat to our life, especially when we didn't feel emotionally safe as children. (That is, for most of us.) It can trigger the survival response and make it impossible for us to think clearly or empathize even with the people we love most in the world.

We have the potential to maintain a higher level of thinking. Between the moment we are triggered and the moment we react, there is a tiny gap in which we have the ability to pause and make choices. We can keep the thinking and empathizing parts of our brains online and choose behavior that is appropriate for our partner or children (rather than a saber-toothed tiger, for example).

Just before our brain switches from the prefrontal cortex (our complex problem solver) to amygdala override (survival mode), we have a moment in which we can mediate the reaction. This moment can be lengthened by meditation and cognitive behavioral therapy, both of which have been scientifically proven to reduce the hyperarousal of the amygdala that develops early in life if we don't feel entirely safe as children.

At the very least, this pause can reduce the intensity of our reactions and the relationship damage they otherwise cause.

In relationships, the fight, flight or freeze response goes

something like this: Something happens. Something is said. Fear around some past event stored in our memory is triggered; our unconscious mind notes that we have been hurt in the past by something that felt similar. We're triggered. Will it be fight, flight or freeze, all equally destructive to a relationship over the long run?

Yet we are reacting to an attack that is not real, that took place in the past, or that doesn't have the power to affect us in the present *unless we let it*.

When we find ourselves pointing out somebody else's flaws or mistakes, we're operating out of our lizard brain. When we operate out of our lizard brain, we're way more likely to trigger the lizard brains of those around us, and things get ugly fast.

It is terribly uncomfortable to be triggered, and without a spiritual practice in place to help ground us, we immediately look to our environment and the people around us as the source of our discomfort. "I was fine a moment ago, and he said X, and now I'm upset and therefore he is clearly at fault." Well, no. He might be, but chances are he is only at fault of triggering something in you that needs to be healed. And for that, he is deserving of your gratitude rather than your wrath.

If we can recognize that we are not in any physical danger in the moment we're triggered, we have an opportunity to find the memory or insecurity that needs to be healed and released. Each time we feel these uncomfortable emotions, we have a chance to heal something within us that is crying for our attention. When we let our triggers control our behavior rather than looking within, we miss that opportunity.

This is what I meant earlier when I talked about my baggage. Our triggers are our baggage. The more wounds we address and heal, the less likely we are to be taken over by our triggers. The less we are taken over by our triggers, the healthier and more loving our relationships will become, including our relationship with ourselves.

The greater our ability to recognize and respond to our triggers, the deeper we're able to understand and love ourselves.

STARTING WITH THE PERSON IN THE MIRROR

Back to me, pregrowth phase: Deep inside, I was a scared little girl who had been hurt. Each painful situation we encounter either builds a wall or pulls one down; as a child, I'd built myself a wall that promised safety but blocked out love and hid the pure, true me away. This disconnection made me insecure, which led to me disliking myself, judgment I then projected onto others.

Naturally, my marriages weren't the only area of my life in disarray. Financially, I was a hot mess. I often went shopping to fill the void I felt within. During my first and second marriages, I also reached for comfort in the form of alcohol and recreational drug use, which brought on superficial feelings of excitement and happiness. That happiness didn't last (big shocker) and then shame would creep back in, making me more depressed and defensive. (And an even bigger jerk, honestly.)

My romantic relationships were a mess, my finances were in turmoil and I bounced from job to job, finding something to be unhappy about at each workplace. I was horribly unstable in my work life and found it difficult to sustain friendships. I allowed the people in my circle to take advantage of me, and then felt even more comfortable sitting in a victim mindset. In my eyes, everything was done to me.

It seemed much easier to point the finger and fault other people than to look at my own reflection and recognize that I was creating my reality through my thoughts and actions.

Eventually, though, a combination of unbearable suffering and curiosity led me to the realization that I was creating a great deal of my own madness. When it finally began to happen, it was a tough pill to swallow. (Yet so freeing and beautiful, too!) I started taking responsibility for my own feelings, actions and reactions. It is truly amazing how much energy is freed up when we release the expectation that others should make us feel a certain way. Eleanor Roosevelt knew what she was talking about when she said, "Nobody can make you feel inferior without your consent."

The truth is that nobody can make us feel anything without our consent. When someone says something unkind to us and we feel shame, for example, it is because they have triggered an inner insecurity, our belief that we may be shameful. When they say something thoughtless and make us feel misunderstood and alone, it is because an inner insecurity has convinced us there is something in us that makes it impossible to connect with other people. When they say something loving and we feel unlovable, we'll find a way to convince ourselves that they're either deluded or insincere.

When these insecurities are healed through self-love, even unkind and thoughtless comments don't land. We understand that the person speaking is having a bad day (or year, or life), and it doesn't mess with our emotional equilibrium. If it does, we shake it off and move on quickly. If someone's difficult behavior becomes a habit, we spend less time with them. We create boundaries and spend more time with healthy people.

LOVING ME

For years, I had cursed my body for not being thin enough; my brain for not retaining what I was supposed to be learning in school; my personality for not letting me fit the mold of complacent daughter, wife and nurse; my lack of drive for not allowing me to excel at anything in life; and me in general for being lazy, ugly and stupid. All that self-loathing was wrapped up in a big bow of shame.

For as long as I can remember, I felt angry that I was never good enough. I would think, "If I only looked like her, everything in my life would be perfect." Or, "If school were just easier for me, then I would be admired." "The thinner I am, the more I'll be loved." From early childhood, I believed I could be saved from my unhappy life only if I was pretty or smart enough, neither of which I ever remember feeling I was. The closest I could ever come was by judging others: I may be lazy, ugly and stupid, but they're worse. But judging others is a boomerang of suffering—as soon as I projected those toxic ideas outward on others, it reinforced that part of my ego that put all of humanity on a sliding scale of wretchedness, and I felt even more fear and shame.

Unhappy and desperate enough to open myself to the teachings of others, I started to realize that a complete lack of self-love was at the heart of all my problems. Afraid, but finally brave enough to be deeply vulnerable with myself, I began by taking tiny steps forward, inching my way toward a positive internal dialog. Standing in front of the mirror, I vowed not to say anything negative about myself or my appearance. I also vowed not to look outward for acceptance in any form. I went with the old saying, "Don't say anything if you can't say anything nice." I avoided the mirror when walking past or getting dressed. I stopped focusing in on my midsection, the place I found most repulsive, and instead focused on the things other people complimented me on. I dug deep and told myself that I had nice calves and skinny ankles. Earth shattering, right?

It wasn't easy, and it took time, but after a month or so, something started to take hold. I realized that it could feel nice to accept a compliment from myself.

Being on the opposite side of self-love—crippled with fear that we aren't strong or beautiful enough, that we'll never be perfect—is incredibly painful. The only path to peace is pushing through the discomfort and learning to love and honor our essential selves: mind, body and soul.

My entire life, I longed to be loved and accepted. It sounds like a cliché, but through experience, I've come to understand that the love we desire and yearn for is right there, waiting—inside of us.

What does it look like to love myself today?

It's learning to honor myself, understanding that I need to forgive myself and to forgive others.

Self-love isn't a perfect picture or the pot of gold at the end of the rainbow. It is an ongoing relationship, learning to listen to the needs of our inner child, our higher self, our ego self and our physical body. It's about learning to honor our dark times, feeling the pain and sorrow that we have all pushed down and numbed with food, drinks, shopping, addiction—whatever coping mechanisms we have. And not judging that!

Self-love is understanding that this whole human life is a process of learning and reuniting with our true selves. Every single one of us has a different version. It is designed that way.

Am I my truest self?? Uh, no! I have days—weeks, sometimes—when I get pulled into a funk or something somebody says really makes me angry or sad. I have to check in with myself and remind myself on a consistent basis that this is a learning experience. I pray and ask for guidance. It is given through lessons, interactions, new people being placed in my life, and some being taken away suddenly or painfully.

Self-love is taking a deep breath, giving myself some grace, knowing I am learning lessons that will lead me toward joy and beauty somewhere along the line. It means being aware that these things aren't actually happening to me but are all pieces of the puzzle of our being.

Being on a journey of self-love doesn't give us a free pass from life's heartaches, but it can help us move through them without being swept away by the riptide of reaction.

If I had to give a concise description of self-love it would be this: The person who stands firm in her boundaries, with love. Self-love is accepting me, right where I am: accepting my past, accepting my present and accepting that I get to play a part in creating my future. It is allowing myself to feel what I feel, without judging myself, without feeling guilty.

SELF-FORGIVENESS STARTS WITH FORGIVING OTHERS— THERE IS NO OTHER WAY

I find it's hardest to forgive the people we care about the most. It is so much harder to think of our life without them, and we have put effort, time, trust, faith and energy into those relationships. Because they know us best, it feels like their actions are commentaries on who we are—they've seen us, they've judged us, and it may feel as if their actions demonstrate their lack of care and approval. When they hurt us, we feel it so deeply. The closer we are, the more vulnerable we become.

We also feel more vulnerable in areas where we have been hurt before, so the painful patterns that often develop in families and partnerships wound us profoundly.

We know we are growing when we can start forgiving our acquaintances (friends of friends, the barista, the guy that cuts you off on the road). Then we start finding it easier to forgive friends and our extended family.

The spiritual guide Ram Dass wisely says, "If you think you're enlightened, just go spend a week with your family." My deepest fear was that I wouldn't be able to make my parents proud. Of course, I know this isn't true now. But it's taken 39 years to get here.

Self-love is reaching the heart of our heart, forgiving others and forgiving ourselves. Allowing a little more grace to our family members allows us to offer more grace to ourselves; allowing more grace to ourselves allows us to offer more grace to the people we love. As we learn self-love, we start to learn that other people's behavior is never a commentary on who we are—they might even think it is, but we're all just mirrors to each other. Hold up a loving mirror to someone and you will both see nothing but love—unless that person is not yet ready to see themselves through the lens of love, in which case they'll question your mirror. Even then, it's not about you.

For me, self-love is finally coming to accept those really dark times that I don't want to think about. The times I felt guilty or ashamed for what I had done. Loving all of me and forgiving all of me.

Marianne Williamson, the Course in Miracles teacher, always talks about, "Giving it to God." All of it. Whatever higher power you believe in. Surrendering to love, forgiving.

ONE DAY AT A TIME

All of this may seem overwhelming. It is a daily, step-by-step process, the work of a lifetime. It isn't a destination but a path. One step leads to another; the results you achieve start to change your experience and perception. You'll begin to experience a sense of opening, of warmth. You'll feel the blossoming of the authentic you.

Self-love is the journey of ultimate forgiveness. The most difficult person to learn to forgive has been myself, especially because I am responsible for the lives of my children.

Self-love is also learning to trust our inner guidance systems.

It's working to be aware of our thoughts, paying attention to where our energy goes and how we feel after interactions with other people. It isn't mean or rude if you don't connect with someone. You don't even have to find a reason. Just allow your energy to direct you where you do feel a connection.

I had a very beautiful encounter several days ago. A gentleman asked me, "How do you let go?" (We'd been talking about emotional baggage, wounds, trauma and anger.)

I replied, "Ah, that is the million-dollar question. I'd love to hear your answer."

"You let go by allowing yourself to feel."

Feel however it feels right to you. Obviously, we can't go punch someone because they've made us angry, but that energy needs to move somehow. Some people exercise to move negative energy, some meditate, some draw, write, paint, do breathing exercises, break things. Teacher and author Tosha Silver writes that she likes to go to Goodwill and buy a whole bunch of cheap plates and glasses; she takes them home, finds a safe place and then smashes the heck out of them. There are even destruction rooms where you pay to take a baseball bat to everything in a secure and safe room, with proper protective equipment. No cleanup required, all part of the admission fee. Feel it and move it, in whatever way feels good for you.

I tend to be more of a meditator and crier. It's a new experience for me to allow the tears to flow and it's taken a long time to feel comfortable crying in front of others. But now I allow myself to cry—it's the way my body likes to release energy. Happy, I cry. Sad, I cry. Angry, emotional, I cry. I have just learned to accept it and not apologize for it. That is a big deal for me. Because even as I write this, I hear a voice from my childhood: "Stop crying. You're acting like a baby." Or, "There she goes, turning on her tears to get sympathy." (Self-love means sending those old voices to their rooms until they have something good to say, too.)

Later in the book, I'll share a valuable tool that I use when I am angry and want to identify the true source of the pain, acknowledge it and allow it to move on.

As I've worked on this book, the growth and evolution of self-love has continued. Even a year ago, I hadn't gotten to the point of slowing down to listen to and be consciously with my body.

This is another stage of self-love. Today I try not to rush and allow my impulsivity to run the show. I try to take at least one deep breath to embrace my present and allow the input to slow, if just for a nanosecond. I choose love as my lens. I honor the way my stomach aches after eating fried food. I talk to it. Maybe it sounds crazy. But it's part of allowing myself to be heard on all levels. Rather than curse my digestive system for hurting after an unhealthy meal, like so many times before, I listen to it. I take in what it's telling me and understand that my body finds it difficult to digest this type of food. My body feels so good because it is being heard and taken care of.

How do you learn to love yourself? There are several strategies that have been invaluable to me in my journey. I find that this work is much like physical activity—you can't do it once in a while and expect to see positive changes. Consistent practice is key, and you have to be patient. Just as with a healthy diet and exercise, change happens when we make it a priority to practice self-love, acceptance and mindfulness every day.

If you commit to even 15 minutes a day of these practices, every day, your life will change in ways you can't even imagine.

→ Educate yourself about self-love and emotional intelligence. There are thousands of self-help books on learning to love yourself. Some of my favorites are:
    a. *Love Yourself Like Your Life Depends on It*
       by Kamal Ravikant
    b. *Dying to Be Me*
       by Anita Moorjani
    c. *Choose Yourself*
       by James Altucher
    d. *Judgment Detox*
       by Gabrielle Bernstein
    e. *The Power of Now*
       by Eckhart Tolle
    f. *Seat of the Soul*
       by Gary Zukav
    g. *Adult Children of Emotionally Immature Parents*
       by Lindsay C. Gibson

If these don't speak to you, there is an entire self-help industry spanning all religions, cultures and languages. Take a walk through your local bookstore or scroll through Amazon and you will quickly find an entire section with many beautiful books by many wise authors. Allow your intuition to guide you to what resonates with you personally.

Watch inspirational videos and listen to inspirational podcasts. If you don't know where to start, here is a list of some of my favorites:

Oprah (duh)	Gabrielle Bernstein
Simon Sinek	Wayne Dyer
Warren Buffett	Mel Robbins
Abraham/Hicks	Kamal Ravikant
Glennon Doyle	Brené Brown
Lisa Nichols	

YouTube is an incredibly valuable resource and it's still free; Oprah's *SuperSoul Sunday* podcast is always a healthy treat.

→ Learn to love your physical form. Look at yourself in a full-length mirror. Make a conscious effort to avoid judgment or discontent. Find your favorite part of your body. Thinking good thoughts about yourself is not egotistical. In fact, our ego is all about fear, so it too is healed and softened by self-love.

Touch your body gently with your bare hands and show love and gratitude to it. Thank it for protecting you, for keeping you free of infection, for your ability to move through the world, for creating your children (if you have any), for calibrating and recalibrating and fixing the harm caused to it. Most importantly, thank your body for keeping you alive. While you look in the mirror, tell yourself:

"I am enough." (Borrowed from Marisa Peer.)

"I love myself." (Borrowed from Kamal Ravikant.)

"I am whole and beautiful the way I am, right this moment."

→ Along the way, you will probably find that you judge yourself and compare yourself to others on a regular basis. As soon as you notice these thoughts, smile toward them and then envision them evaporating like clouds. Gently do this as many times as you need to, without judgment. These kinds of thought patterns are hardwired in us, a genetic inheritance from generations of ancestors who would die if banished from their tribe. But in today's world, they are harmful to our happiness and relationships. Thank them for helping your ancestors live long enough to create you. Now let them go, off to the land of the ancestors. Remember that your walk and journey are yours alone. Nobody will ever travel the same path or see the same way you do. If you constantly compare your experiences to those of others, you will never fully understand the value in your own lessons. And until you do, you will keep receiving the same lessons, over and over in different forms. (Which is why this book's title isn't *1st Time's the Charm*.)

→ Filter the negativity in your life. Doritos are delicious, but you wouldn't eat them every day and expect to produce a healthy body. Negativity in the world around us is similar—a sometimes-tasty toxin. For now, I urge you to stop watching news and reality TV. Stop reading newspapers and gossip magazines. Stop filling your mind with the drama that seems to fill each social media channel. Listen to music that makes you happy, not angry. If you have that constantly complaining friend, take a break.

The suffering of others should not be our entertainment. We only have so much energy in each day, and it is our responsibility to protect it and direct it in ways that support the life we want to create for ourselves.

➤ It's also important to check in with yourself every time you spot a negative thought or judgment aimed at others. When this happens, I try to ask myself, "Why is something someone else is doing or saying bothering me? What's going on with me right now that needs some self-love and attention?"

Which brings me to the most important tool of all:

➤ Look in the mirror and acknowledge that you are creating your reality, right now and always. When you can shift your perspective from seeing everything being done to you (Why did this have to happen to me?!) to recognizing that you are constantly cocreating your life (Where is my opportunity to grow here?), it is astonishing to see what happens next.

When you are upset with someone, ask for a timeout and look within. Why does their behavior trigger you? Chances are it's because you have an unresolved issue that you haven't yet dealt with or healed.

One of my favorite quotes, used by many transformational speakers and authors, is: "Your outer existence reflects your inner state of being." Another beautiful question we ask in our home on a regular basis comes from Wayne Dyer: "What comes out of you when someone squeezes you?"

Is it love? Is it anger or frustration? Why do you feel this way?

The other possibility is that your emotions are telling you it's time to give yourself some self-love by setting boundaries. If you've given yourself time to get calm, examined your response to ensure you're not experiencing an old emotional baggage trigger, and still find you're not okay with the other person's behavior, it's boundary time.

You can choose to put boundaries around the amount of time you spend with this person or around how you interact with them. Sometimes you just have to keep it super-superficial and time-limited, as with that aunt who can't stop herself from making inappropriate comments around your children.

If this is someone who is a non-negotiable presence in your life (like your partner or your manager at work), talk it through. First figure out what need of yours isn't being met. Then start your conversation from a place of vulnerability. "I am feeling hurt and I need your help." (At work, you may want to replace this with "I am feeling [disappointed, confused, etc.] and need your help.) Next, make a request for the behavior you do want. Note that, for this to work, your request cannot be a threat or a demand. The person you're talking to must know that you will continue to be respectful and caring toward them even if they deny your request. For example, "I feel that my need to feel safe and respected isn't met when you are yelling at me. Would it be possible for us to take a cooling-off period and talk when we're both calm?"

→ Practice gratitude: Being actively, consciously grateful starts you off on the right foot each and every morning. As soon as you open your eyes, make a mental list. What you're grateful for can be as simple as the bed, couch or floor you slept on, a blanket over your body, or that you opened your eyes today. The purpose is to focus on what is positive and meaningful in your life. The more you focus on the positives, the less power life's negatives have to overpower and control your mind. It isn't easy, but you can shift your thinking patterns. With consistent effort, you can develop new neural pathways that will become your default position. Eventually, it won't be an effort to make a positive choice. It will just come naturally. This ability of the brain is called neuroplasticity, and it really is the secret to creating a happier, healthier, richer life.

You'll find that the transformational speakers and authors I mentioned earlier practice gratitude each day. As one Redditor put it on a thread about life-changing realizations, "Gratitude *is* happiness." Imagine—happiness is the product of simply looking toward the blessings in our lives, even when they are limited.

As soon as my eyes open, I thank God/Source/ Universe for gifting me with another day of new possibilities. Along with my husband, I usually have a child or two in my bed who migrated there sometime during the night. I offer thanks for their health and well-being, for a roof over our heads, for financial freedom, family, friends and anything else I can think of.

This practice helps me remember how blessed I am each day. I encourage you to do this too. I can promise you that your life will begin to bloom in ways you can't imagine.

This is the whole of what I know about self-love right now. Like me, I hope you'll start learning more every day. We can learn together.

Each one of the lessons that follows is something that was essential in transforming my marriage. But none of them would have made a difference without self-love. It is the oxygen in every relationship as well as the key to health and happiness in each aspect of life.

Your Three Transformative Questions

In an ideal world, how would you like to be loved by a partner? Take as much time as you need, and without lifting your pen from the paper or your fingers from the keyboard, write about the ways you'd like your partner to express his or her love for you. Next, write for as long as you need to about the ways you'd like an ideal parent to love you.

....

....

....

....

....

....

....

....

Do you currently treat yourself the way you just described? If not, what has to change? Spend as much time as you need writing about the way you'd talk to and treat yourself if you loved yourself the way you'd like to be loved by a partner and a parent.

....

....

....

....

....

....

....

....

....

....

....

....

What is the single most influential change you can make today in order to make yourself feel more loved? (Yes, by you.) Is it self-forgiveness for things that happened in the past? Learning to love your body for the way it serves you as opposed to the way advertisers say it should look? Choosing friends that contribute more positively to your life? Learning to set healthy boundaries and hold them? Whatever it is, write a commitment to yourself, in your own words, to make this change. "As of today, I will .... If I make a mistake, I will forgive myself and start again."

....

....

....

....

....

....

....

....

....

....

MARRIAGE IS A PARTNERSHIP, NOT A COMPETITION

Nearly every person I have spoken with about being unhappy in their marriage automatically begins with a laundry list of things they do, and their spouses do NOT do.

Let's get this out of the way right now.

If you want to be happy in your relationship, it is time to stop looking at the things your partner doesn't do and start appreciating the things your partner does! No matter who you are, there are things your partner does for which you are not giving him or her credit.

Hard medicine, I know. It would be so much easier if she did more, or with less grumbling, or you just had a few more minutes in a week for yourself. Or if he just appreciated the things you do a bit more.

What if I were to tell you that gratitude is the single most powerful way to change that balance in a positive way? Many studies have shown that expressing our appreciation inspires more of the behaviors we want. As for the behaviors we don't want, the same studies show that a neutral response is best. In other words, don't even notice.

More importantly, a happy marriage is not a series of transactions. There are times in each relationship that one partner needs to give more than the other.

Today, rather than looking at our marriage as a balance sheet, with my contributions in one column and his in the other, Jay and I work at seeing things as a true partnership. There is just one column. Some days, he puts in more effort, and some days I put in more. But that doesn't mean we can start carving out notches and keeping score. Quite the opposite.

I'll never forget the day that my outlook on marriage changed forever.

We had been doing well in our relationship for a few years at this point, and we were watching the 2016 Summer Olympics. There was a feature story on beach volleyball star Kerri Walsh-Jennings. The news anchor asked several of Kerri's close friends what she was best known for in their group. Unanimously, the answer was, "She is the most amazing wife."

I was stunned. Stopped in my tracks. The inspiration hit me in the head with a hard thud. When asked about this response, Kerri replied that her goal each day is to be the best wife and person she is capable of being.

It made me realize I wasn't living up to my potential as a wife, partner and person. This was the moment—sitting in my cool, dark basement, watching the Olympics—that my entire perspective shifted.

All bets were off the table and it no longer mattered what anyone else outside of my marriage thought.

I believe this is when our marriage became fully aligned with God/Source/Universe. Once I set my intention and made a conscious effort to give the absolute best I could spiritually, emotionally and physically, miracles began showing up regularly in our life. I gave my best version of me to my husband, without expectation of receiving something in return. Without the desire to get acknowledgment from my peers. I did it because I had a "holy instant," as Gabby Bernstein calls these moments.

I recognized that I respected my husband enough to do the work to release my old baggage and fears. I surrendered to love. I learned how to love unconditionally, all trusting, all deserving, fully exposed, with my heart wide open. Amazingly, I began receiving the love he always had been trying to give.

By surrendering in this way to one other, we found our flow; it allowed us to put our marriage above all else, above all situations and certainly about anything that could potentially harm our union.

Negativity and people and situations that caused drama in our marriage began to fade away.

About two years before this marital awakening, Jason and I had a discussion about moving forward or calling it quits. We were both at the end of our rope with the way we were thinking and acting.

My ego had taken over. There was very little about our

marriage that I saw through the lens of love. I was irritated by the smallest things, like having to wake Jay up in the mornings. (It's now one of my favorite things to do.) I saw our life together as a competition and I was always keeping score. I was ugly, and he was giving. But I knew he was getting tired of giving so much.

As we sat on the couch having a serious discussion about our future, we agreed that we wanted to try and work things out once more. But we were going to do it differently this time.

We made a commitment to each other to surrender to one another entirely and really put our best into each other and our marriage. We discovered *The Love Dare* by Alex and Stephen Kendrick. We went through the entire book and did the daily exercises. It took 40 days. It was not easy a lot of the time, but the beautiful thing was that, each day, my heart softened. I began to realize that I had carried the baggage of my childhood, previous painful experiences and my failed relationships into our marriage. I had allowed the influence and opinions of others to enter our marriage.

And I realized I didn't want to continue in the same way.

Once the walls around my heart began to fall, I began loving myself and forgiving myself for my past, present and future. I had to work all the baggage and self-loathing out of myself. I fully accepted that I had to stop looking for happiness in the arms of others or in externals like shopping and eating.

I had to love myself first, before I could receive the love that was lying right next to me each night. And once I really accepted that love ... well, now we can't do enough for each other.

Your Three Transformative Questions

How would you describe the partner you'd like to be in an ideal world?

....

....

....

....

....

....

....

....

....

....

Are you that partner today? If not, what has to change?

....

....

....

....

....

....

....

....

....

....

....

....

....

....

LESSON 2

What is one easy thing you can do today to move closer to your ideal vision? Do it, without any expectation of it being noticed or appreciated.

From now on, each morning when you're brushing your teeth, make a point of choosing one more small, easy-to-do act of affection. Then put it at the top of your to-do list.

Finally, put a time on your calendar three months from today to write about what's changed in your life as a result.

....

....

....

....

....

....

....

....

....

....

....

YOU GET TO CHOOSE YOUR PERCEPTION OF YOUR LIFE

Other than self-love, nothing is more critical to a good life or a good marriage than understanding that the way we interpret our reality *is* our reality. We get to choose whether we view our life from a perspective of negativity and judgment or from the perspective of love and gratitude.

Life becomes so much better and more joyous when we begin to focus on the positive, loving moments in our day-to-day interactions with our spouse, coworkers and the world.

If you haven't picked up on it yet, I happen to be a big believer in what's often called the "law of attraction." Jay prefers to call it "clean living." It doesn't matter what you choose to call it. It means that, when you focus on negative, you attract more negative. When you focus on positive, you attract more positive. You don't have to think of yourself as a spiritual person to recognize that negative people are drawn to negative people and positive people are drawn to positive people.

If you want more positive experiences in your life, you must look for the positives in every experience and interaction. Yes, even the challenges! And you must go through your life with good and positive intent. You need to want to do good and be a good person.

After I say my morning expressions of gratitude and prayers, I slowly rise from my bed. My feet ache and my muscles and joints begin to work out the stiffness of multiple sclerosis. I thank God for the ability to feel my feet. It's a big deal, because I couldn't feel them for about six months. I thank and honor my body for carrying, protecting, healing, balancing and maintaining homeostasis, and for keeping me alive.

I sit in meditation for at least 30 minutes and am steadily growing my meditation times. While I understand that meditation isn't the answer for everyone, I've learned that I need it to slow down the inner chatter of my mind. I notice that if I don't take that time each day, I become bogged down with disorganized thinking and anxiety due to the compounding to-do list that will otherwise grow infinitely.

Maybe sitting in the lotus position focusing on your breath doesn't work for you. But find something that slows your inner dialogue and allows you to be with yourself.

Meditation for you could be a walk in the park or listening to comforting music for 15 minutes. Find an activity that teaches you to be an observer of your thoughts and actions and commit to it. Life gets so much easier when we realize we are not our thoughts, emotions, reactions or even our bodies. As Eckhart Tolle writes, we are the consciousness that watches our thoughts, emotions, reactions and our bodies. The ultimate freedom is being able to separate ourselves from the reactions our body is experiencing to the degree we can comfort and calm ourselves.

I encourage you to carve out time each day to spend within yourself. This is where you learn to be comfortable with you. This is where you begin to realize that you are the master of your thoughts and your perception of the world. (Your thoughts may initially be like wild horses, impossible to soothe, but given time and practice, you'll get better at it and they'll get tamer.)

It's common knowledge that we live in a world of chronic overstimulation. Throughout my spiritual journey, I've learned that checking in with myself through meditation is the healthiest and most effective form of soothing my otherwise hyperaroused amygdala and aligning myself with God/Source/Universe.

Centering, listening and just being is essential to my mental health. Putting this time first on my priority list means I don't take out my fear, anger, stress and anxiety on my family. I have experienced the results of allowing fear and ego to take the wheel in my relationships, and I'm committed to doing whatever I have to in order to make sure it doesn't happen again.

As I write this, it's a cool February morning here in Arizona. Years have passed since my string of failed marriages.

It's also been years since the challenging time I described that Jason and I faced and overcame together.

I sit in our quiet house, the kids at school, a sense of peace and calm throughout our home. I look at Jay with gratitude and love that makes my heart feel as if it could explode. I feel honored to be the first face he sees each morning. I feel blessed beyond words that I get to be the first human interaction he has every day.

I am humbled to be able to provide my husband and kids with positivity and love each day before they leave the house. I strive to be the best wife, mother and person I can be and to smother each member of my house with an awesome amount of love and happiness. In turn, I know they can go out into their day and do the same.

I keep in mind that the way I wake my children and husband will have a direct effect on the type of day they have, so I do so with the intention of easing them happily into their morning.

Of course, as any mom or dad knows, we have our routine early morning struggles, unexpected breakdowns and temper tantrums. Children wake up tired and shoes go missing. My goal is to not get sucked into the stress, to—as I sometimes think of it—find the joy in the shit moments. It is a challenging goal for anyone except maybe the Dalai Lama. But note that the goal isn't to find joy in the shit moments—it is to try.

I have observed that if I set this intention, I set the tone for the type of day these beautiful people, the most important people in my life, will have. I want them to feel safe, comfortable and enough (in every sense of the word) in our home and out in the world. This is their sanctuary as well as mine.

It has taken many years and "get back up and try again" moments for me to learn how a healthy marriage operates. I've had to learn to build lifelong communication skills and a thriving partnership.

Along the way, I've proven to myself over and over that the way we choose to see our daily life and marriage is one of the most influential factors in our happiness and the happiness of those closest to us.

People don't often pay attention to their perception of life. I hear so many people talk about how much they dislike or hate parts of their life or even their whole life. Before I began this journey, I was the same. I just didn't know that I had a choice—that I could control my thoughts and emotions to the extent that it would change my perception of this life, and through my perception, my happiness.

I usually wake up without an alarm clock around four. I use early mornings to check in with myself during meditation, taking time to write, reflect and say affirmations. To "fill my cup." I set out clothes for our younger boys, pack their lunches, fill their water bottles, wake them up, get them in the shower, and then gently wake my husband of more than 10 years. He usually keeps the kids on task with school preparation as I make breakfast. After breakfast, I assist with toothbrushing, hairstyling and shoe tying. I walk the kids to the door, kiss them and wish them a good day.

I turn to my amazing husband and kiss him goodbye.

To some, this is a dream. To others, it might sound like hell. For me, this is my heaven because it is all I ever desired. According to the statistics—as a person from a broken home who grew up witnessing failed and abusive relationships, who suffered abuse as a small child and adolescent, and who had my own failed marriages—I shouldn't be where I am today.

Seven years ago, I was pissed off at my husband for not getting his lazy ass out of bed to help me get the kids ready for school. I took offense at his failure to jump up when the alarm went off with a gleaming smile and can-do attitude. I muttered shitty comments under my breath about how I was busting my ass while he was snoozing away.

Perception is truly a gift from God above. It is completely individual, and nobody will ever perceive life the same way you do, but you do get to choose.

Slow down for a second and really think about the following statement:

The way you choose to perceive your life is the core component, the foundation, of your life. Your perception can create a smooth, grateful and joyous life or an angry, sad and dark life.

You get to decide. We are so blessed to have the power to completely change our lives with nothing more than thought.

A SHARED VISION

Use your imagination and daydream about a beautiful partnership with your spouse. If you don't like the word daydream, use the word visualize.

Visualization is a technique used by top athletes, actors, speakers and many other public figures. They do this for several reasons. First, science has shown us that the brain has limited ability to distinguish between imagining an activity and performing it. The theory behind this method of training is that neuropathways are established through visualizations, making it easier to perform the task in real life.

The second theory is that this practice aligns with the law of attraction: visualize the outcome you want, and you will attract it. I happen to think throwing in a nice prayer helps too. But that is my opinion.

Whether you believe one, both or none of these theories, if it works for top performers, it should work for us too. Why not try it? While writing this book, I did a daily visualization of sitting down each morning with a cup of coffee, asking my writing guides to assist my fingers as they tap quickly on the keyboard. Two things happened: my brain become conditioned to the act of sitting down to write after my early morning routine. In just a few short months, it become engrained within me. I have developed a new habit or neural pathway. If I don't sit down to write, I feel off. Additionally, I firmly believe that we attract more of what we focus on. The more I sit down and write, the more excited I am that I get to do it each morning. Even if I sit down and have no plan about what I should be writing at this moment, I see the work I am putting in. I see the word counts grow. I see my investment in time and effort growing and I am becoming proud of my work. I am emotionally invested. In return, Universe/God/Source continues to guide my hands and provide me with experiences to share.

This can be true for all aspects in our lives. Each morning when you awaken, after you finish your morning affirmations and gratitude list, take a few short minutes to visualize the interactions you would like to have with your spouse during the day ahead. There is nothing limiting your visualization or imagination. Visualize your partner waking up kind, gentle and caring. Imagine yourself waking up the way you did when you spent your first nights together.

Things don't always go the way we want or imagine because there are so many working parts. But at some point, what you imagine and visualize will manifest in your life if you are doing it with the right intentions. Same goes for the opposite end of the spectrum: if you constantly worry and send out fearful energy, you will attract those things that you are consistently thinking about.

Albert Einstein said it best: "Your imagination is your preview of life's coming attractions."

Imagine or visualize the relationship you desire with your partner. While you are imagining, feel the feelings as though it is happening right now.

When you were a young child, did you daydream? I remember playing make-believe a lot. When I played Barbie, I imagined my Barbie mansion, pretending all day long that I lived in this beautiful home with the husband of my dreams. Jem and the Holograms performed at my pool parties. I could throw one hell of a party at the age of six. It was fun, imaginative, creative play. That's the kind of daydreaming I am talking about here—joyous, hopeful and present, with good and pure intention.

Imagine your perfect day before you begin your regular day. Do you have a lot of tasks to complete that you want to go smoothly and easily? Do you want to have a stress-free morning? Do you want your kids to get along? Do you want 10 minutes to yourself to collect your thoughts? Whatever you desire, imagine it.

In the words of Abraham, speaking through Esther Hicks, once you imagine and desire an outcome, the universe knows your desire. This knowledge then sits in your creative vortex, the energies that surround you. As soon as you have learned whatever lessons you need for your soul's growth in the place you're in, these outcomes will begin to appear in your life.

For me, it seems that these outcomes appear once I become fully emerged in my present life, after I take inventory of all the amazing things I already have. Abundance just doesn't flow into a place of negativity. If I want something because I don't have it and I feel envious that someone else does, I won't receive it. Or, if I do, it will be part of a lesson—the outcome will be short-lived or cause a ridiculous amount of trouble in my life. This is why intention is so important.

Intention is like the breath of life. It is your true lifeline. If you have negative intentions with your visualizations, it will lead to bad energy coming back to you. Of course, we have all had negative intentions at some point in our lives. We are human, and it is part of our ego's genetic design. When we are hurt, our first reaction is often a desire for revenge. An eye for an eye, right? When we feel judged, we want to "show" people—we may want something not because it's true and right for us but because we want to impress others. Or we may visualize an outcome as a way to avoid the hard work of self-love and forgiveness. Needless to say, these kind of intentions bring us new lessons rather than the outcomes we're dreaming of. Wayne Dyer left us with so many beautiful quotes during his life, including this wisdom: "How others treat you is their karma. How you react is yours."

The same goes for every aspect of our lives. Our good intentions are powerful tools that create beautiful waves of positivity in our lives. When you want the same joy for the whole world that you want for yourself, you will find that everything comes more easily to you.

Combined with our thoughts and imagination, intention is the key to accessing what we desire. It is also the only thing that stops the ego, which otherwise takes us to some strange places.

When my ego steps up, I find that I will say something and, within a few seconds, I will ask myself, "Why did I say that?"

"Oh, maybe I shouldn't have said that."

"Shoot. Did I say something inappropriate?"

Intention stops all of that chatter. If I can recognize that my ego is chattering in my left ear, then I can ask myself, "What was my intention?"

If my intention was positive, well then, it's all good. I can tell my ego that my intention was for the highest good of all and really mean it—my karma is good!

What is your intention when visualizing a beautiful marriage? Do you want a deep connection with your partner? Do you want to fill your cup and be with someone whom you love to sprinkle with the joy that brims over? Do you want to be a safe space for your partner?

I will share my intention with you as a place for you to start thinking about your own. Please remember that it will change over time and that I'm not suggesting that your intention should look like mine.

My intention for this time in my life is to be the most authentic version of me. My intention is to love myself unconditionally and to love my husband and children unconditionally, exactly where they are in this moment of their lives. I want my family to feel loved, safe, secure and enough in all aspects of their unique selves. My intention is a prayer for the highest good of everyone I encounter.

Now, when I imagine my day before it begins, I have this amazing intention that puts my ego to rest and allows my higher self to visualize the best day I can imagine. Some days I visualize sailing on a private yacht off the coast of Greece with my kids being educated by well-educated tutors. Calm, cool and collected, we explore the world and learn through our exotic experiences. I can see the clear blue ocean water. I can see my healthy, happy husband, beaming with a big smile of delight and peace, basking in the sunshine.

Some days I imagine we are living in Northern California, in a beautiful home with panoramic views of Muir Beach and the wild ocean off the Pacific Northwest coast. I can even hear the freighters gliding past the lagoon. I see myself standing at a kitchen island, in my workout pants and a baggy sweatshirt, sipping my coffee after doing yoga on my screened-in deck. I can feel the cool, early morning mist from the ocean, see the velvet grey sky. I imagine my kids happily at school, hubby in the office working, in our quiet and peaceful home.

Today, I visualize waking up, my body strong and healthy. I imagine the kids waking up happy, excited and rejuvenated from a great night of rest. I imagine them getting ready quickly and peacefully, enjoying their day, laughing and having fun. I enjoy my husband being peppy and happy as he leaves to take the kids to their summer class. I visualize myself having a great deal of energy and getting all the housework done, laundry folded, kids picked up from class, beautiful afternoon swimming, enjoying each other's company, a nice dinner and movie, followed by the kids peacefully being tucked into bed and going to sleep right away.

You can visualize whatever you want. That is the beauty of daydreaming.

Of course, the day doesn't always go as planned or visualized. In my visualization, it was a great day from start to finish. My actual day didn't go as planned at all. Jason started the day with an emergency tooth extraction. So, I had to take the kids to summer fun class, Jay ended up taking the day off work, and I had a neurology appointment I had forgotten about. However, a few of my visualizations did go better than planned and one event, my neurology appointment, went exactly as I'd visualized it six months before.

Before my last regular appointment with my MS specialist, I visualized him saying, "I don't need to see you for a year," at our next appointment. In my visualization, my health had bounced back, and I was feeling fabulous. It was a not-so-believable idea even a year ago. Multiple medications had failed to help, and my MS was progressing, with worsening symptoms. I remember wanting so badly to be free from illness and not wanting to spend the money on visits, scans and tests, not to mention the time and energy. I was over living in chronic disease and worsening illness. I had felt hopeless for some time.

However, I hung on to a sprinkle of faith that all would work out the way it was supposed to. I surrendered to my illness, just as I surrendered to my husband and marriage. I accepted it for what it was and decided to make the best of my situation, right now. I focused on the things that I could change—most importantly, my mind.

My health didn't change overnight, and I would be lying if I said that visualizing changed it by itself. In my experience, that's not the way visualization works—instead, it opens our minds so that we are quicker to spot solutions that ultimately make the difference. With the help of my medical team, I eventually found a medication that is working beautifully with my body. I had to commit to investing my time and effort in staying positive and looking at what I could change. I had to become even more aware of how my thoughts were affecting me and the people around me. I had to recognize that my body could no longer tolerate the way I had been treating it, just as my marriage could no longer tolerate the way I was treating it five years earlier. It was then that I could begin to make small changes in my behavior and intention and act consistently in ways that benefit my health.

It took months for me to get to the visualization of my doctor saying "See you in a year!" rather than "See you in three months."

I visualized to the point where being healthy became a familiar feeling again. I had to go through the darkness to really appreciate and recognize the magnificent work my body has been putting in during the 39-plus years since my conception.

I've often had to take two steps forward and one step back. There are times in all of our lives when we have to step back in order to gain perspective and see the lessons we've been given. Now, I appreciate my middle-aged body more than I have appreciated any of the many versions of my body I've known since birth. I know now that better health is a precious gift we can give ourselves. Even when we're tested by the most intractable illness, there is still a lot we can do to be our healthiest self within the boundaries of our condition.

In losing and regaining my health, I learned the healing value of joy, authenticity, love, commitment and faith. As I learned those lessons, my health improved, and now I protect it with the tools I have been given. My health and well-being began moving in a positive direction when my thoughts and visualizations started moving in a positive direction.

The same rules apply to marriage.

I don't deny it can be much more challenging when another person is involved in your process. At least with my health, I could control what I was saying, and the internal struggle was something I could do in the privacy of meditation and journaling. I know that, often, our partner may also be fed up and tired. They have their own perceptions, expectations and desires—their own visualizations of a perfect day. This is what makes us all so wonderfully unique and gives partnership the potential for such richness.

We may have to learn to hold two visions, one for ourselves and one for our partner, and hold onto faith that there is a way to meld those two sometimes very different outcomes. We have to accept one another, to send love and positivity out into the world through our thoughts, imagination, visualization and intent. As the Buddha taught, joy is accepting what is given to us; suffering is the inability to accept that same reality.

If you can get the momentum of your thoughts and visualizations moving in a positive, uplifting direction, you will begin to notice the changes. You will even become more aware of the times when your visualizations manifest right before your eyes, as they did for me during my last doctor's visit.

The vision of a healthy, happy, loving marriage will guide and inspire your actions, moving you in the direction of manifesting the relationship of which you dream. But because the same is true of negative thoughts and visualizations of betrayal, it's essential to be aware of your thoughts in the same way that you're aware of what you eat.

Accept where you are right now in your relationship and figure out what you can do to make it better. Don't focus on what you cannot fix or change. Just let that go for now. Remember the Serenity Prayer: "God grant me the serenity to accept the things I cannot change, the courage to change the things I can and the wisdom to know the difference." Here is a helpful tip about knowing the difference: the things you can change are within your skin; everything else is outside of your control.

One small step at a time gets you moving. If it's in the

right direction, you will eventually get to the top of life's mountain, with all its stunning views.

Along the way, don't forget that life is not the mountain-top but the moments of your journey. The power to move forward comes from our appreciation of the beauty around us right now, right before our eyes, even in our darkest hours.

Your Three Transformative Questions

What would have to change in order for you to be truly happy? Make a list.

....

....

....

....

....

....

....

....

....

....

What would you miss about your life today if it was all taken away tomorrow? Fill as much space as you can on the next page.

....

....

....

....

....

....

....

....

....

....

....

....

....

Are you willing to try turning your focus from the shortcomings in your life described in the first list to the blessings you've described in the second whenever you find yourself focusing on problems? How might doing so change the way you feel?

....

....

....

....

....

....

....

....

....

....

....

....

....

BOTH PARTNERS HAVE TO BE IN THE MARRIAGE

I have been in a marriage I didn't want to be in; I felt I'd made a mistake. I have also been in a marriage in which my husband felt I was the mistake.

Fortunately, I'm now in a marriage my husband and I both want to be in. We've held fast to our commitment to one another.

My first husband was very invested in our relationship, but I was too young and needy. I couldn't see his needs because my own were screaming. I didn't have the tools to create a successful union, nor did I really care. I thought I knew it all and, boy, was I wrong.

We both did things that weren't great for our relationship. His biggest issue was that he was a heavy spender, unable to say no to pretty much any impulsive purchase or expensive decision. I was the same way, and we dug ourselves into such a financial mess that the sheer strain led us into a tailspin of ugliness.

He tried very hard to make things work, but, looking back, it's clear we didn't have the experience, understanding and tools to overcome our impulses or cope with their outcomes. Neither of us knew how to put our partner first, but I know now that he gave far more to that marriage than I did.

I found his opposite in my second husband. His insecurities convinced him he had to manipulate me and isolate me from family and friends. He was disrespectful to everyone we encountered. In this environment, my own darkness emerged, and I became an angry person. He poured gasoline on my insecurities and we both burned with anger, sadness, disappointment, rage, judgment and shame until there was nothing left of our relationship.

He was fully invested in his own survival and I allowed him to take from me until I had nothing left to give.

I did everything I could think of to make him happy, including things that compromised my integrity. It took a while for me to understand that I could never do enough. It was devastating to finally acknowledge that I thought so little of myself I let it all unfold, that I hated myself so much I allowed another self-love-deficient person to make me the target of his inner demons. In that process, I became a destructive person in the lives of those around me.

My third husband was an innocent bystander during my second divorce. He was a coworker and we had a relationship that should never have turned into marriage. Husband number two and I, with kids in tow, had moved out of state, away from my family, friends and any type of support. Husband number three was close by when I needed help numbing the pain and grief of my divorce. He helped me get off the couch when I was so depressed I didn't think I would survive.

He asked me to marry him after a very short courtship and I felt an unhealthy sense of obligation. I was such an emotional and psychological mess that I wasn't making clear decisions and plans. I was in no state to date, never mind marry. I felt terrible for pulling him into the shitstorm of a life I had created.

I learned the hard way that like attracts like.

I guess you could say that he helped me rediscover my truth. When he began displaying some alarming, irrational behaviors, something happened in my mind. A light turned on and I woke up. I could see clearly, in a way that I never had before.

One evening, while he was in a fit of rage, I began to have a clear view of where my life path was headed, and it terrified me. I had this realization during a violent moment; I was trying to stop him from bloodying his own face.

It became clear to me: these were not my inner demons to fight or fix. My world slowed down, and in that moment, I knew that I was not making the best decisions for myself or my children. I recognized that this was a critical point of choice in my life. Our union lasted a short few months.

I remember being so afraid of how others would see

me when I told them I was divorcing, again!! Rather than nurturing and loving myself out of grief, I shamed myself and projected my shame into imagining how other people might shame me. Shame on me! Shame on ME!

WHEN YOU LEAST EXPECT IT

I was about to receive a lesson in the way the universe seems to catch us when we listen to our inner voice and take a leap of faith.

One week after I had my wake-up moment, my beautiful sister and her family came to town for a spring trip. We had a lot of sister talk time, and I confided what was happening in our home. It was a blessing that she was there with me that week and helped me get my mind clear and focused.

Through a series of events that only God could orchestrate, I met Jason, my brother-in-law's best friend. It still blows my mind that we could have met countless times in the previous years and never did. We both thank our lucky stars that we didn't meet earlier, when neither of us was ready.

The first moment our eyes met, I knew he was going to be a big factor in my life. It wasn't like, "OMG!! He is so hot! I want to hook up." It was a deep, heartfelt sense of reunion. I knew from that moment that my life was never going to be the same.

I spoke only to my sister of my feelings and swore her to secrecy because I knew I wasn't ready; I had just filed for my third divorce. I didn't want yet another relationship to start for the wrong reasons.

Jason is a gentleman and honored my need for space and time for healing.

With time apart, alone, in a quiet house at night, I began to heal the inner wounds from my past. I began to play with my kids and have fun. I started really working hard. I knew that one way or another, I needed to get my shit together for them.

Eventually Jason and I started dating—or what I think of as courting—and nine months after that, we decided to get serious and move in together.

To me, Jason was and is a breath of fresh air. He was literally the first person I dated who had his life together. Once I committed to getting my life together, someone who had his together stepped into my life. Again, like attracts like.

He didn't need me to pay his bills, or drive him to school every day, or teach him how to be a nice human being. He didn't need to be fixed. He is a good man, kind and respectful even when he doesn't think anyone is paying attention. He has never said things to hurt me or make me feel inferior. He never wanted to tear me down. But the most alluring thing about him in those early years was that he made as much of an effort to get to know my kids and form relationships with them as he did with me. He took us all on dates; my older boys adore him.

I honestly still struggle to figure out what Jason saw in me back then. It makes me want to laugh and cry at the same time. I can now see it was a transformational time in my life. I was taking the first steps away from allowing my past to define me and toward taking action to change my story. I realized that I had to take care of my business and obligations before I could commit to him fully. Maybe he saw my strength. Because, looking back, it took some serious strength to pull myself out of the hole I had dug myself into.

Now, that isn't to say that my previous baggage just disappeared. As mentioned, I had a lot of work to do on letting go of it. I still have triggers and I still work to manage them, and to manage and reduce the intensity of my reactions when they occur.

It took me several years of being married to Jason before I got a full understanding of marriage as a partnership. Together, we have done a lot of studying and learning. We attend church and read books. We put the tools we picked up along the way into practice together. I have had therapy. A lot of conversations, grace and experiences have brought us to the true understanding of partnership.

As in all relationships, we have challenges and obstacles in our marriage. We are human and have arguments from time to time. I do things that irritate him and vice versa. The quality of a relationship is defined not by avoiding these scenarios—which is impossible—but by how we treat each other in addressing them.

I have heard so many times over the years that marriage is a 50/50 partnership. Experience has taught me just the opposite.

If you both give 50 percent, your marriage will reach a maximum of 50 percent of its potential. Both partners must want to be in the marriage, and both *must put in maximum effort.* That is not to say that you have 100 percent of yourself to give each day. Of course not. Life happens. We are human beings living in a busy, materially driven society. There are ups and downs, job losses, health issues, the deaths of people you love. Etc., etc. None of us is immune to life's challenges.

These are the times when the one partner can and should step up and take on more than the other. This is the partnership! We both give 100 percent of what we have to give.

Sometimes that 100 percent is not much, but rather than kicking your spouse when he or she is down, try responding with understanding. Try responding by *giving more*. Look at the circumstances surrounding their day. Is there something going on? Did he have a rough day at work? Were the kids making her want to pull her hair out today? Was there bad news? Curiosity and understanding are powerful tools in all relationships.

We only have so much energy each day; sometimes that energy is taken up by demands we aren't even conscious of. As partners, one of the most powerful things we can do for our own happiness (and that of our children) is to recognize when our spouse needs to be uplifted and given some grace.

There will be a time in your life that you will require the same support, if not more. Trust me. It will happen.

Aside from the day-to-day trials and tribulations of life—raising children, dealing with family members, life and life's issues—I have seen so many people fall ill and need to rely on their partners, myself included.

I was diagnosed with multiple sclerosis in January 2016. I like to call this time in my life my pre-awakening. Looking back from where I am now, it's hard to think about how negatively I treated myself and those around me. The societal rat race? I was all in. I thought I had to conquer the world and prove that I could be a successful mother with well-adjusted children while being a successful nurse pushing for the top, continuing my education, maintaining a spotless home, and shuttling kids to and from school, practice and extracurriculars. Oh, and keeping up appearances for those around me.

I was still trying to prove to the world (and myself) that I was not a failure. I took medication to help keep me thin, I overexercised, and my inner dialogue was terrible. It's really not a surprise I ended up getting sick. (But that is another topic that I might just find myself writing about in another book.)

The point is, how could I have been there for my husband when he needed my support? Let alone recognize his needs? The answer is, I couldn't have. I was committed to so many things that gobbled up the energy that I could have otherwise put into my marriage and family.

The beautiful thing about losing your physical health and mobility is that it gives you a lot of time to think. For the first time in my adult life, I needed someone to physically care for me. I had never even imagined that happening. I was the nurse, the one who cared for and healed the sick. It's humbling when your family must carry you upstairs to your bed because you can't walk.

I was able to observe my husband being my caregiver. As a nurse, I am very keen about noticing compassion fatigue. I watched for it in him and, if I am totally honest, I expected it. Everybody gets tired of taking care of others at some point—that is just the cold hard truth. Why do you think there are so many studies and research done on healthcare workers and compassion fatigue and burnout?

Yet Jason never burned out. He never threw his hands up and said, "I need a break." My amazing husband stood up to our vows: "in sickness and in health."

He carried me when I needed it and when our marriage needed it. He gave 100 percent of himself to our marriage for more than a year. He took care of the kids when I couldn't. He got them fed and their lunches packed. He took care of me, drove the kids to school, took them to practices and movies. He did everything on my list, plus his own. He never complained. He never moaned. But most importantly, he never carved notches or held any of what he did for me against me.

He just said, "That is what we do!"

It reminds me of a beautiful verse by the poet Hafiz: "Even after all this time, the Sun never says to the Earth, 'You owe me.' Look what happens with a love like that—it lights the whole sky."

Your Three Transformative Questions

If you think about your marriage as a third being in your home, are you and your partner nourishing it enough to keep it growing and thriving? Or just enough to keep it alive? Or is it slowly dying?

....

....

....

....

....

....

....

....

....

....

Are you and your partner both committed to a healthy future for your relationship?

....

....

....

....

....

....

....

....

....

....

....

....

....

If you see your marriage as just surviving or slowly dying, are you willing to get help to make your future together better? If so, get couple's counseling if you can. If not, I recommend starting as we did, with *The Love Dare*.

....

....

....

....

....

....

....

....

....

....

....

....

....

....

....

GRACE TRANSFORMS MISTAKES INTO WISDOM

We are all human beings!! In a world in which economic growth is driven by telling us we need improvement now, it's so easy to forget that the one thing that connects us is our humanity. Being human means that we each have a completely unique brilliance, gifts we're given to serve the world. In this way, we are all completely different. The thing we have in common is that every single one of us has made mistakes and will make mistakes again—in this way, we are all exactly the same. (Isn't it beautiful?)

In my earlier marriages, we had a general theme of bringing up each other's past mistakes and transgressions during each argument.

Dredging up the past to keep reminding your partner they made a mistake is extremely unhealthy. It's unhealthy for your partner, but even worse for you.

I understand that many mistakes can have a tragic effect on trust, love and marriage. Depending on what you have endured, forgiving may seem like an impossible challenge. But you cannot move forward while living in the past.

It is self-torture to keep recommitting to the pain of past experience.

You must make the choice to forgive everything that has or has not occurred. If you really want to be happy and healthy, from this moment on, you must forgive.

You must let shit go!

Forgive yourself!

Forgive your partner!

Choose to forgive together and work together!

Take the valuable lessons that mistakes are here to teach us human beings and learn from them. Because if you don't learn from your mistakes and change your actions, the same circumstance will keep coming up in your life until you do.

You'll never stop making mistakes—but if you're growing, they'll be new mistakes, and you'll manage them with increasing grace and resilience.

When your partner makes a mistake, look in the mirror at yourself and evaluate your reaction to what happened and why. I understand this can be as difficult and serious as infidelity and as minimal as picking up the wrong showerhead from the store. (Flashback to an episode of *Jon & Kate Plus 8*, in which she is screaming like a lunatic over his erroneous showerhead purchase.)

If your marriage is a masterclass in love—and it is—the mistakes you and your spouse make are the exams. They'll tell you what you still need to learn.

Your Three Transformative Questions

Are there things in your past you haven't forgiven your partner for? Can you forgive them now?

....

....

....

....

....

....

....

....

....

....

What are the things you are afraid you haven't been forgiven for in your relationship? Are you willing to ask your partner for their forgiveness? (Don't mistake forgiveness for amnesia. Trust is a difficult thing to rebuild and takes time.)

....

....

....

....

....

....

....

....

....

....

....

....

....

Is it possible to treat each other with the grace you each brought to your early relationship? Take as long as you need to write down the characteristics of that early relationship and what you loved about it.

....

....

....

....

....

....

....

....

....

....

....

....

....

YOU KNOW WHAT'S BEST FOR THE KIDS? LOVE.

Growing up, I saw very few healthy marriages.

My parents divorced when I was a baby, and I saw my dad every other weekend.

I never wanted to leave my dad because, before he met my stepmother, he made me feel secure. He lived with my grandparents and we spent most of our weekends with them. It was one of a very few places I felt safe.

Unfortunately, it would be short-lived. My father remarried when I was three. In the years that followed, I was exposed to severe drug abuse, alcoholism, absurd dysfunction and abuse that took years of therapy and self-help to overcome.

I learned quickly that if I spoke of the violence in our home, I was labeled a troublemaker. The wrath we faced after telling someone what was happening was far worse than taking the abuse. My brother called child protective services multiple times and the system failed us, time and time again.

Learning to love myself has meant learning to forgive my parents for their mistakes, learning to understand that they were doing the very best they could with the limited tools they had been given in their own childhoods. I know that they loved me and love me still. But I now also understand that this is where my own insecurities and feelings of inadequacy began. I felt *inconvenient* and my ego began trying to protect me at a very young age. It was nobody's fault, but it was real, and it left me with a lot of healing to do.

Sometimes divorce is better for the kids. If there is emotional or physical abuse, you owe it to yourself and your kids to get out of the situation any way you can. (Get help— many women stay because they know that leaving can also be dangerous.)

When I was going through my divorces and someone would ask, "What about the kids?" my ego would reply with a defensive "They'll be better off because they won't grow up with parents who hate each other."

This statement assumes there are two choices: staying together and behaving badly toward each other or divorcing. If you really want to put your children first in your decision-making, know that you and your partner have to learn to behave respectfully toward each other. We've all seen situations in which the incivility between the ex-spouses gets worse, much worse, after the divorce. It's horrible for everyone involved, but it is worst for the kids, who love both of their parents.

If you find yourself in this situation, if you and your partner can't seem to stop bringing out the worst in each other, get help. Get help with the same urgency you would if your house was on fire. Because you are teaching your children everyday how to have relationships. And if you are teaching them how to have unhappy, shaming, disdainful relationships, you are setting them up for future misery.

There are three primary things that you can do to future-proof your kids against bad relationships. First, learn to love yourself and be happy. These are skills they need to learn from you. Secondly, learn how to have healthy, respectful relationships. By learning to love yourself and have healthy relationships, you will achieve the third essential, providing an environment in which your children feel safe, loved and welcome.

There are so many studies about divorce and its negative impact on children. What is harder to quantify is the impact of emotional violence on kids, that is, when people stay together and treat each other badly because they're so unhappy.

Ask yourself the following questions:

 » Are you being disdainful or dismissive to your partner in front of your children? (Ask yourself this: Would you be okay with your children acting toward you the way you are acting toward your spouse?)

➤ Do you act civil but cold to your partner and pretend there is nothing wrong when you're inwardly burning with rage? (Your children can feel that shit, even if they don't know what to call it.)

➤ Do your children see you acting emotionally out of control? Are you regularly "losing it"?

➤ Do your kids know they can come to you when they have problems? Or do they sense you're too consumed by your own?

➤ Are they constantly anxious that your family and the only home they know are in danger of disintegrating?

➤ Do they so desperately want you and your spouse to get along to the degree that they are either functioning as small adults or acting out to change your focus?

Losing our cool and saying or doing things that are destructive to our relationships is something that happens to all of us.

When I'm triggered, I find myself reaching for sarcasm or worse, hurting the people I love most in the world. It's a pretty common scenario—as we talked about in Lesson #1, we're all predisposed to this kind of all-out reaction when something wounds us or makes us feel threatened. If these kinds of reactions happen too often, the damage piles up, and after a while, our partner is walking on eggshells around us or withdrawing completely. Or we find ourselves withdrawing, doing everything we can not to upset our partner even at the cost of our happiness and the intimacy within our relationship. Too much cut-off and we're now in a situation where it's easy and natural for one or the other partner to start seeking emotional connection elsewhere.

LOSING "IT" AND
FINDING IT AGAIN

The problem with being triggered is that we really "lose it"—that is, we lose our ability to think clearly and manage our behavior.

Let me get a bit science-y on you for a bit. It may seem as if I'm getting off track, but believe me, this has everything to do with transforming your relationships and creating an environment where your kids feel safe.

In one of the largest studies of its kind ever conducted, the Adverse Childhood Experiences Study conducted by Kaiser Permanente and the Centers for Disease Control and Prevention in the mid-1990s found that traumatic childhood experiences are common:

» Almost 40 percent of 17,000 participants reported two or more adverse childhood experiences (ACEs), defined as physical, sexual or emotional abuse; physical or emotional neglect; exposure to domestic violence, substance use disorders or mental illness in their home; their parents' separation or divorce; or someone they lived with going to prison.
» More than one in 10 people (12.5 percent) experienced four ACEs or more.
» The study found that ACEs tend to happen in clusters: only 13 percent of participants who reported adverse childhood events had experienced only one, while the other 87 percent had experienced two or more.

The study also found that ACEs have a "dose-response relationship" with psychological, physical, behavioral, social and emotional disorders later in life. The higher the ACE score, the greater the likelihood of high-risk behaviors such as smoking, substance use disorders and promiscuity. High ACE scores also correlate with severe obesity, depression, heart disease, cancer, chronic lung disease and a shorter life.

When compared to people with no adverse childhood experiences, participants in the study who reported four ACEs were found to have a seven-fold (700 percent) increase in alcoholism, a doubling of cancer risk and a four-fold increase in emphysema; six or more ACEs is associated with a 30-fold (3,000 percent!) increase in attempted suicide.

In other words, childhood trauma doesn't just affect us emotionally during our childhood—it affects us throughout our bodies and throughout our lives.

It's worth highlighting that this study used ACEs as a way of measuring the experience of childhood trauma. But trauma can be defined as anything that overwhelms our ability to cope; trauma occurs when we feel that our life, our sense of self or our connections to people who are essential to us are in danger. In childhood, we are entirely dependent on the adults around us, so we see their behavior and their responses to us as critical information about our future survival.

The experience of adverse events isn't the only way children can be traumatized. If we were anxious by nature, if we didn't feel loved by our parents because they were often unavailable to us emotionally or physically, or if our parents were unable to cope emotionally or practically with their lives, we grow up feeling unsafe. In other words, the vast majority of us have experienced childhood trauma that affects us physically, mentally and emotionally throughout our lifetimes.

Mark Wolynn, an expert in inherited family trauma, refers to a 35-year Harvard University study that found that

100 percent of participants who described their relationships with both their parents as "tolerant" or "strained and cold" were diagnosed with a major health issue in middle age, compared to 47 percent of participants who described those relationships as warm or close.

Before you feel the need to defend your parents or blame them for any of your current health or relationship problems, I'd like to point out that if there is one thing that defines and unites humanity (beyond making mistakes), it is our love for our babies. You can be absolutely sure that your parents loved you as much as they were capable of loving and did their best for you, even if their best was terrible. As the title of Wolynn's amazing book, *It Didn't Start with You*, implies, the childhood trauma we experience is often sourced in the trauma the adults around us experienced as children, and that their parents experienced as children. There is no one to blame, not even ourselves. We're all doing the best we can. But by becoming conscious about the sources and effects of our own childhood trauma, we can free ourselves as well as our children. If they are still alive, our healing can even help heal our parents.

In *Waking the Tiger: Healing Trauma*, clinical psychologist Peter Levine writes about an impala running for its life. As a tiger lunges, escape impossible, the impala drops to the ground as if it is dead. Somewhere in the impala's DNA there is a memory of an ancestor that was able to escape when a tiger left it unguarded for a moment, thinking it was now a dinner that could be delayed for a more convenient moment. Even if this opportunity doesn't present itself, the freeze mechanism means the impala is now protected from the pain it would otherwise experience.

In Western culture, we hear a lot about the "fight or flight" responses, but perhaps because of our action-oriented culture, the third, equally common response to a perceived threat is often left out. An animal that cannot fight or flee will freeze.

Just like the impala, we are born with hardwired responses that take place outside of our conscious minds. In our modern world, the threats that feel the most dangerous to us are not usually wild animals, but threats to our sense of self-worth and belonging.

As children, we are like impalas who cannot run. If we don't feel safe in our homes with our parents, flight or fight are not options. In one way or another, we freeze. We lock in emotions that desperately need to be processed. We develop defense mechanisms that are our immature minds' best efforts at creating safety. These mechanisms range from closing ourselves off from others so that affection can't be used as a weapon against us to relying on immature outsiders for our sense of safety and self-esteem (joining gangs or becoming sexually promiscuous) to cutting ourselves as a way of distracting ourselves from emotional pain we can't control. We may become extra "good"—learning to be hypervigilant and hyperresponsive to the needs and emotions of the people around us, discounting our own needs—or hypercontrolling, manipulating others in an attempt to feel safer.

Whatever our locked-in emotions and outdated coping mechanisms are, what they have in common is that we are largely blind to them. They are frozen inside our bodies, in our unconscious minds and nervous system. When something reminds our unconscious of a childhood trauma, we are triggered, and these frozen emotions and defense mechanisms hijack us. We can't access our thinking brains or empathy; we are flooded with the hormones that drive the physiological fight, flight and freeze responses. In these moments, we may even find ourselves doing something to destroy a relationship so that our partner cannot hurt us by leaving.

The more profoundly we experienced trauma as children, the more easily triggered we are. An offhand comment, a well-meant but clumsy attempt to help, a new cologne our partner applies before going out with friends—all may be triggers that are impossible to explain. When we're asked to explain, even to understand ourselves, our psyches reach for something global and generalized that makes sense: "I know what you meant!" (Better than you know yourself!) "You have no respect for me!" (No one respects me.) "I can't trust you!" (I can't trust anyone.) "What do you expect?!" (In fact, this kind of global, nonspecific language is one of the best indications we've been hijacked by a trigger situation.)

It gets even more complex. In the last 10 years, scientists such as Rachel Yehuda at the Mount Sinai School of Medicine have discovered that our childhoods could be perfect in every way (if that were possible) and we can still experience these kinds of latent trauma reactions. Her research team discovered that trauma causes changes in DNA that are passed onto the next generation. In other words, we can be triggered by things *that relate to our parents' trauma*. Since her discovery, research in mice and rats has found that these genetic changes can be passed on to a third generation and possibly more. Even without specific triggers, these DNA changes can set us up for further trauma by, as Mark Wolynn describes it, turning our stress dials up to 10. A highly sensitized nervous system means we are always on guard, never fully relaxed, and more prone to interpret the actions of others and situations around us as threats.

Children with this kind of genetic inheritance are more

likely to experience trauma themselves as a result of their high levels of sensitivity and anxiety. When they grow up, their likelihood of finding emotionally healthy partners is reduced. They are more likely to damage their relationships by being triggered more often and acting out in destructive ways when triggered.

It isn't easy to break this cycle, but it is possible. As mentioned earlier, cognitive behavioral therapy and meditation are both proven ways of resetting our nervous systems, lowering our stress dial to give us more time between experiencing a trigger event and reacting to it. Even an additional three or four seconds can give us time to say, "I'm feeling triggered. Let's talk after I've had a chance to process these feelings."

Meditating just 10 minutes each day will change the way you experience triggers and will soon give you more freedom to regulate the way you react under stress. More meditating, more freedom.

If we have children, we love them. (If you don't have children, I'm guessing you've already skipped ahead.) One of the most rewarding things we can do is to put love in action by doing everything we can to reduce our triggers and improve our relationships skills. Read John Gottman and Marshall Rosenberg. Watch their YouTube videos; read or watch anything by Brené Brown. If you can afford it, get couple's counseling. If you can't, consider going to Al-Anon or Adult Children of Alcoholics/Dysfunctional Families together. (There are almost always drugs or alcohol in the picture somewhere when we inherit these relationship dynamics. It is natural to seek comfort in oblivion, even when it isn't healthy.)

I know this from a child's standpoint and a divorced single

mother's standpoint. It is a hard pill to swallow; it certainly was for me. It forced me to look at myself and my actions, without excuses or justification.

Once you learn how to relate effectively in an intimate relationship, you may still want to get a divorce. If so, you'll be able to get one of those divorces that put the children first and don't leave them with years of emotional damage to heal.

I have had to deal with many situations with my older boys, who are now 19 and 15, that were direct effects of the ways their fathers and I treated each other before and after divorce.

My younger boys are now eight and six, and they're being raised by their biological parents in a functional, loving, committed relationship. Needless to say, the challenges they face are very different.

My older two have struggled with learning to navigate between parents who weren't emotionally mature. They've had to witness a lot of dysfunctional behavior.

As I've said before, this work is not easy. It is hard to look at yourself and face your deepest, darkest fears. But we must investigate our own darkness to get to this place of acknowledgment and recognition in which the darkness can be illuminated. All the freedom and joy in life is on the other side—for us and for our children.

Are you in a situation where you feel justified in leaving? Or that you have to leave? I get it! And I have left. I can tell you this for sure: you won't regret it if you allow your children to have some say in what is occurring in their lives. Take the time to listen to them and ensure that they come first in your decision-making, above all else. It's the reality of being a parent—self-love requires that you do what's best for your children and yourself. You can't separate their well-being from your own any more than you can hurt their other parent without hurting them.

Your Three Transformative Questions

Is there something you need to change in order to give your children their best chance at a happy relationship as adults? If so, are you willing to start the work?

....

....

....

....

....

....

....

....

Go back in time and ask your child self what she or he learned about relationships from the adults in your life. What would you like to unlearn?

....

....

....

....

....

....

....

....

....

....

....

....

....

What would you like to teach your children about love?

....

....

....

....

....

....

....

....

....

....

....

....

....

....

STEP-PARENTING.
IT'S HARD.

L et me rephrase that. Parenting is hard. Step-parenting? It's a minefield.

It takes years of trust-building to discipline children effectively. If you are a step-parent, remember that disciplining them is not your job. It is the job of their biological parents. There are times when you need to back up and allow the bio-parents to handle situations with their children, even if you are sure you know better.

Until you've had a chance to accumulate those years of trust-building, and sometimes even then, it can be helpful to think of yourself as a step-friend. You can be a wonderful role model and support person.

Finally, whether you are the ex-spouse or the step-parent, remember that when you are talking badly about your child's other parent, you are attacking someone they haven't completely individuated from yet. That is, they think of their parents as part of themselves, and when their parents are attacked, they suffer. Don't do it.

I know emotions run high when dealing with an ex. The more you've been hurt, the more intense the emotions. But do everything you can, including getting counseling, to avoid getting sucked into negativity and drama. (If you're finding yourself in this situation regularly, you may want to go back to Lesson #1 and Lesson #7 and revisit the information on triggering and how to interrupt it. Even in this, practice makes ... well, progress.)

If necessary, think of your relationship with your ex as a business connection. For the sake of your kids, emotions need to be in check. You must stay in the part of your brain where you can problem-solve effectively.

Have a strategy prepared for moments you find yourself triggered, such as when you feel attacked or criticized. You're modeling excellent emotional intelligence to your kids when you say, "You know what? I'm feeling triggered and not myself. Let me process this and get back to you."

Sometimes that's too much to ask of ourselves. In those moments, practice smiling as a yoga pose. Put a small, closed-mouth smile on your face, even if it feels like a mask, and say nothing. Move through the moments, keeping the smile in place. It will calm you.

I still work on these skills regularly. It wasn't until a few short months ago that I was able to take back all of my power and see the fathers of my older boys simply as human beings, just like me, trying to make their way in the world. They make mistakes, just as I do. It took me 15 years, with many arguments and ugly words, thoughts and feelings, expensive lawyers and far too many tears before I learned to release the past, present and future. I sat in anger and fear for so long. All it did was create more anger within me. Once I finally asked God to help me see through the eyes of love, once I prayed for my exes and sent them all the loving energy I could conjure up, my heart began to soften. I was able to release and be free of them emotionally.

I felt like I could breathe again.

In a recent situation, when my ex's new wife questioned one of my decisions and then said some hurtful things, my response was, "I am sorry you feel this way."

It was a moment of transformation. I finally recognized that I had the opportunity to choose differently than I had in the past. I sat back for a moment and realized that I am okay with not being friends with my exes or their new wives. As Gabby Reece once said, "Thirty-three percent of the world will love you, 33 percent will hate you and 33 percent doesn't care about you." It is okay that my ex-husband's new wife sees me through his eyes.

Then I prayed for myself and for them. I prayed for God to help me see this situation through the eyes of love. It was then that I saw me, the 21-year-old me, in her. I also saw that this is her journey. I prayed for God and the angels to hold a space of love and healing in their marriage and for their children, including my son.

Once I did this, the anger subsided. They no longer have

control of my emotions, whether it is fear, anger, resentment, or just frustration. They no longer have the power. I took it back through prayer and by seeing the situation through the eyes of love. (I'll probably have to take it back again sometime, and that is okay, too.)

Jason, on the other hand, has been so patient. It has been his role-modeling that's taught me how beautiful a step-parenting relationship can be. He has been a consistent, reliable and secure adult in the lives of my older children for 11 years. They know that Mom does the disciplining. The only time Jason jumps in is to say: "Your tone is getting disrespectful. I don't allow anyone to talk to my wife in this manner. I suggest you tone it down or take a break." That is all that has ever been needed. Of course, our family has had screaming matches, arguments and disagreements. We aren't always the most mindful of parents. But we are consistent, for the most part, and the boys know where Jason stands. I believe this gives them a sense of kinship, friendship and mutual respect for one another.

There have been difficulties bringing our blended family together. But Jason has never tried to take the place of their fathers. He has loved them from his space, the space of a supportive, loving stepfather. He never insisted the kids call him Dad. He never pushed or forced his way into the space I have with the boys. I believe this has made their relationships flourish.

My oldest son is now 19 and in his first year of college on the East Coast. His relationship with Jason is beautiful. They often have late night conversations; they laugh together, they hang out together when he's home, and they are good buddies. I noticed this trend toward a mutual friendship way back. Kids don't just give anyone that type of relationship.

So, I know this type of step-parenting works.

When Austin was 15 or 16, Jason would often come to me to prepare me for a conversation that was coming. Austin would ask him how to approach me in certain situations, mostly when he was going to get in trouble.

My 15-year-old, Kole, was four when Jason and I married. Their relationship is a bit different, perhaps because Kole's bio-dad lives more than 1,000 miles away and never really tried to maintain a relationship with his son. Kole looks to Jay as more of a fatherly figure. I love that he feels loved by Jason.

I highly recommend some sort of therapy or mediation for blended families. At the very least, get on the same page as your partner. Know what you are willing to accept, what support you need as a parent and what you both might expect from the ex-spouse.

Finally, remember to stay in your lane and really work on managing your triggers so negative emotions don't set the tone.

Your Three Transformative Questions

If you are a step-parent, are there ways in which you haven't been staying in your lane? If so, are you willing to stop doing that now?

....

....

....

....

....

....

....

....

....

....

When you're step-parenting, there are two questions that often get mixed up together:

→ Are my needs being met?
→ Are this child's needs being met?

It may feel as if there is a pie that is being divided between you, and that the child's serving reduces your serving. If this describes your feelings, how can you act now to meet your own needs, knowing that children are wholly dependent on their parents and don't have that choice?

....

....

....

....

....

....

....

....

....

If you are a parent (bio- or step-) in a blended family, make a list of three things you could do this year to help improve your child's relationship with their other parents.

....

....

....

....

....

....

....

....

....

....

....

....

....

....

YOU CAN FALL IN LOVE AGAIN!

I understand that, if you are reading this book, it might be a bit much to ask you to imagine yourself and your spouse completely, passionately in love with one another again. That is okay. I am not asking anyone to jump from level one to level 100 by reading a few pages in a book.

I am asking you to take a different approach in your thoughts. I keep bringing this up because every ounce of happiness that you seek in your life, love, relationships, marriage and career is 100 percent dependent on how you perceive your environment, situations and circumstances.

For example, if you wake up every morning to your annoying alarm, and your first thought is, "I hate my job. This is going to be a terrible day," chances are good you are going to have a terrible day. Additionally, everyone around you will be affected by your negative energy. The same concept is true in your relationships. If you are constantly paying attention to what you perceive as being wrong in your relationship, you will keep reliving the same unpleasant scenarios over and over until you stop.

In *The Love Dare*, the authors discuss maintaining space in your heart—rooms, if you will—one for negativity and one for positivity.

The more time you spend in the positivity room, the more you will notice subtle changes. Then, as if by magic, the positive begins to overshadow the negative. The writing on the wall becomes so big and bright that you can't help but pay attention to the awesome positivity.

Spend time each day in the positivity room, even if you can't seem to find very many pleasing qualities in your spouse at first. Start small, if you must. But start. You don't have to do it for your spouse—this exercise will benefit you even more than it benefits the people in your lives.

I know trust can be shattered. I have been on the giving and receiving end, spanning all ranges of the trust spectrum, from the severity of infidelity to the innocent omission of truth. I also understand that most of the world has felt similar crushing blows in a relationship.

Yes, the past hurts. But if you and your spouse are serious about fixing your broken union, you must clean up the mess from within. Clear the clutter to start fresh. In other words, you have to let it go.

Imagine that your relationship is a home, built on a foundation. Early on, it outlasts the storms. You have a lock on the door to protect it from intruders. You have windows and a roof to provide protection from the elements, even though the storms still blow outside. Now, imagine that foundation was poured on uneven ground. Over time, the foundation of the house begins to crack.

The walls begin to crack and the windows leak whenever it rains.

Now a hurricane comes through and destroys your home and everything in it.

In the same way, your relationship begins to crack under the pressure of ego, fear, anger, jealousy and mistrust. The storms and hurricane are choices you have made. The foundation is a lack of self-love.

After the storms, we must clean up the mess and remove the debris to rebuild. But now we know that we need to ensure our foundation is built on solid ground. We learned a lesson: the way we were living was suboptimal for the life we want.

This was one of the most difficult challenges I have endured in my life. I have rarely felt as vulnerable as I did when I finally acknowledged the clean-up and rebuilding that was required to make our marriage work. It's why I say both you and your partner need to be serious about working together.

This phase takes trust and vulnerability. It requires patience. The process must be honored and respected.

I am a living testament to its effectiveness. Love can be rebuilt. Mine was.

You must agree to leave the past in the past and step forward into the light of love together. Show each other grace, love and dignity. Commit to each other and ask one another for forgiveness. Change the behaviors. Forgive. Let the past go.

It's okay for things that upset you to come up in your thoughts. That is your mind's way of letting you know it's still bothering you. The important thing to remember is your reaction. If a thought of something your spouse has done that upsets you comes up, acknowledge it, thank it for presenting itself and give yourself permission to release it. It no longer serves your highest purpose, your spouse's highest purpose, or your marriage's highest purpose. Let the emotion come up. Don't resist or push it back down. Visualize a snapshot of the memory without reliving it. Thank it for showing itself to you and let it know that you are ready to heal yourself and choose your reaction.

Don't be afraid to choose wrong. God/Source/Universe will make sure you get as many chances as necessary to make the decision that serves your best you. Eventually, we realize that the right answer, the best decision, is always forgiveness and love. This is so important. Now we can let it go. Watch those thoughts evaporate like clouds.

The only way to release yourself from anger and fear is forgiveness and love—this is the fresh start on which to build your relationship's foundation.

When you allow yourself to live in anger, fear, regret or anxiety, you dull your shine and the light you naturally shine on your relationships. When you allow yourself to be stuck in the past, you are not giving the best of you to anyone, especially yourself.

Take this one step at a time. Our brains are very good at remembering every situation or event that hurt you; the brain's main job is to protect you from threats. Your neuropathways have been deeply engrained, experience after experience, day after day, year after year.

It takes great consistency to rewire those pathways from fear to love after we have been hurt. It takes time to regain trust and love. Be gentle with yourself and your spouse. If you both put forth the effort, you can move from the pain and suffering to a place of love and beauty.

Real love is built on a foundation of respect, for yourselves, for each other, and for the two of you as a couple.

Next, disregard all your expectations of your partner. Yes! I mean all expectations.

Respect the space and the rebuilding process. Take the time to find and use the highest-quality materials—that is, to treat each other with loving kindness and build new, beautiful memories.

When you rebuild with the highest-quality elements—trust, faith, compassion, and most of all love for yourself and each other—there is absolutely no need for expectations and conditions. This is not a deal, or a series of transactions that must be negotiated. It is a sacred trust: I cannot be happy unless you are happy, and I know you feel the same.

I had a very dear friend ask me, "How do you get the butterflies in your stomach, the excitement of the new relationship, back in your marriage?"

My reply to her was, "You can't. But you can get something so much better."

Let me explain. Each relationship has a series of seasons. When we meet someone, we feel so excited at the newness of the relationship. You can stay up all hours of the night talking, texting and daydreaming about your life together. You have fun traveling together and exploring your new life and each other together. Every relationship has an infatuation phase.

When Jason and I finally kissed, I felt an electricity from

my lips to my toes. It was something almost unexplainable. We talked on the phone for hours at a time. We both had endless amounts of energy and all that mattered was spending time together, completely in the present moment, hoping and praying time would stand still.

Infatuation is a wonderful and exciting time in every relationship.

As I sit here writing this chapter, words from the pastor at our previous church are ringing in my ears. Pastor Scott talked a lot about marriage during his sermons. One Sunday, he was talking about this very subject and about how attachment to the infatuation phase often gets people in trouble in their marriages. Often, when a couple speaks of losing their "spark," they are speaking of this infatuation burning out.

They want to look for that spark. They want the excitement back, and often they begin to look elsewhere for it. He went on to discuss how infatuation is NOT love. It is a good feeling. It is brain chemistry that makes us feel momentary euphoria. And it is 100 percent temporary. When we grow secure and comfortable with each other, it always grows into something else. The goal is to grow and evolve infatuation into love. Love is something so much deeper and more meaningful than the excitement of infatuation. (And yes, you can recreate that excitement, that passion—it just requires intention, imagination and respect for each other. Oh, and time. And privacy. And enough sleep.)

If we can learn to embrace the fact that the infatuation phase is something that will always evolve into something stronger, it gives us insight into how to fall back into love.

Love takes time to cultivate, nurture and grow. It is built by sharing your happiest, saddest, most vulnerable and embarrassing times along with your glory and successes. In short, it takes experiences together for that love to grow into a beautiful marriage.

Before we discuss love and the kinds of experiences that grow love, I feel the need to address self-love again, this time in the context of infatuation. Infatuation can feel and act like a drug—it temporarily cures us of all ailments.

So, when you are longing to bring back a spark back into your marriage, when you are longing for infatuation—ask yourself what you are missing within yourself.

When we're feeling dissatisfied with our relationship, it is often not our partner we're dissatisfied with, but with the way we feel. Infatuation makes us forget ourselves—it is literally a chemical brain cocktail that creates euphoria, reduces our inhibitions and makes us more courageous. It eases anxiety.

If the only way you've ever felt this good is during the experience of infatuation, it is easy to believe you'll never feel this good again without infatuation. But I'm here to tell you that, by practicing the principles in this book, you will feel so much better. And it will be a stable, long-lasting feeling. Not permanent, of course. But sustainable.

The key is learning to feed all your emotional needs yourself. Relying on external factors to bring you happiness, joy and connection makes you needy, too needy to be a real partner over the long term. The more you can find love within yourself, the more capable you are of coming from a place of absolute, unconditional, no-expectation LOVE in your relationships! Can you imagine the power in that?

Love is waking up to your spouse, morning breath and no makeup, knowing that they cherish you even with all your flaws and imperfections. Love is standing over a casket, holding hands and supporting your partner at the funeral of someone they love dearly. Love is the middle of the night pep talk through screaming babies and dirty diapers, or your partner raising you up when you can't bear to get out of bed because of depression or illness.

Love is all-encompassing. Above all, love is understanding.

We must accept that the infatuation phase was a beautiful time in our relationship that blessed us with sweet memories before it faded, leaving us with a wide-open space in which to grow true, long-lasting love.

I understand this can be very difficult, especially where damage to the foundation has occurred, especially where we have to learn to offer love to ourselves while we are learning what it means to really love another.

Here are the action steps. Do them, one at a time, and it will work out, I promise.

1. Make time for each other every day. If you've been daydreaming of something better outside of your marriage, now is the time to stop. In the best-case scenario, you'd simply be taking yourself back to square one and starting your lessons all over again. You've made a commitment to God/Source/ Universe, yourself, your spouse and the state of your holy union. It's time to put your fears aside and honor those vows.

2. Court each other, and each other only! Make your partner the center of your attention, without the expectation of anything in return. When your attentions are dismissed or your intentions distrusted, let your partner know you understand and keep courting.

We all want to belong. Many inspirational speakers talk about this primal need. This is no different within the confines of marriage. Reconnecting is essential. We all need to feel that we are worthwhile and have purpose in our relationship. Even when we have learned to love ourselves, we want to feel loved and cared for by our significant other. We want to feel that our efforts are appreciated.

3. Even if your spouse is not treating you the way you want to be treated right now, begin to set the tone for your relationship by treating them the way he or she wants to be treated. Do something nice without expectation of something in return. On your way home from work, grab his favorite drink or snack. Leave her a nice little message on her windshield in the morning. Make his favorite meal unexpectedly. Send a sweet text saying you are thinking of them and appreciate what they do for you.

When Jason and I began doing this with each other, I worked night shift at the hospital, and he worked day shift. So, it was easy for me to stop on my way home from work and pick up his favorite breakfast, warm and ready for him to eat as soon as he got in the car for work in the morning. It was a simple gesture on my part. But it made him feel that I was thinking of him and did something nice that I wasn't under any obligation to do. Also, don't underestimate the power of a note. Jotting down your feelings on paper and expressing your gratitude for one another is a beautiful way to let your partner know that you have pure intentions and to reaffirm your commitment to your marriage.

I'm not going to lie. In the beginning of our marriage reconstruction, it was tough for me to set my ego aside and just do nice things for Jason. It was difficult for me to think and see from a place of love because I was coming from a place of fear. Why should I do this for him? Shouldn't he be doing it for me?

We had to make the decision together to give our relationship our all and really put forth the effort to put our differences aside, for the sake of growing our love and finding comfort and ease in our marriage.

Those little acts of unnecessary kindness begin to build a connection. The connection will eventually weave its way into the solid foundation you are building. They become bigger acts of appreciation and gratitude, which begin to grow and develop trust, with positive, pure and loving intent.

For this to work, your gestures must be an offering, not a transaction—meaning, you cannot perform these acts with the expectation of receiving anything in return. And more importantly, you cannot harbor expectations about how they should be received.

When you expect a certain kind of reaction, you are giving with the intent to receive something in return. By definition, that is not a gift. It is only when we give more than we take that we begin building something that lasts.

Your Three Transformative Questions

When you think back to the earliest days of your relationship, how would you describe the way you felt? Excited? Special? Open-hearted? More alive?

....

....

....

....

....

....

....

....

....

Are there activities you can do with your partner that might bring some of those feelings into your relationship today?

....

....

....

....

....

....

....

....

....

....

....

....

....

....

Do you plan your dates with your partner with the same care and anticipation as you did at the happiest point in your relationship? If not, what needs to change?

....

....

....

....

....

....

....

....

....

....

....

....

....

GET ON THE SAME PAGE FINANCIALLY. P.S. THE SAVER IS RIGHT!

Money is always a tough topic of conversation, especially when two people have different opinions and beliefs about spending, saving and investing.

Whatever your beliefs are, both partners need to be heard. An agreement needs to be made between the two of you about your budget (yes, you need a budget, but I find it helpful to think of it as a financial freedom plan) and saving for the future, regardless of your financial status.

I have seen so many marriages struggle, and ultimately fail, when money troubles arise, including my own. For some reason, most of us are very territorial with our money.

"It's mine; nobody should take it from me."

"I should do what I want with it."

"Nobody should tell me what to do with it."

"I contribute. I should be allowed to spend what I want."

These are all thoughts that I have had myself. Most of the time I thought like this, my net worth was negative. I can only imagine how those with larger incomes might feel!

Money is a tool. While it can make life less restrictive, it will never make you, me or anyone else happy. Nor will the impulsive shopping sprees and hyperconsumption of unnecessary stuff.

When you view money as a tool, it becomes possible for you and your partner to work together to achieve that tool's optimal performance.

Money isn't love, although it can feel like it. And it isn't self-worth, although it can feel like that too. It isn't safety or security or even freedom. It's a tool—that's it. We have to learn not to hold it so personally.

When I begin to feel overwhelmed with financial thoughts, it helps to remind myself that money is much like a hammer. We are working to save and make decisions that will upgrade our hammer to a nail gun. When I think of money in such simple terms, it takes away the pressure and the personal attachment.

We should absolutely honor our financial commitments and we should work together to tackle whatever financial strains we face. We need to be responsible and prepare for our family's future. It can be hard, especially if we're addicted to the relief of shopping therapy or if our income isn't stretching to cover our basic essentials at the moment. But I'm here to tell you it's possible to free ourselves from shopping addiction, to make it through those difficult times, and that sharing goals can even make the journey exciting and fun.

If you and your partner establish a plan and stick with it, at the very least, you will be on the same page. This will eliminate the arguments about your different points of view.

In *The Total Money Makeover*, Dave Ramsey says that couples must tackle their finances together. If you chose to have a lifelong partnership, you have to be able to make financial decisions together. Even if you maintain separate accounts and incomes, your money decisions will have a direct impact on the futures of your spouse and children.

Generally, each relationship has a spender and a saver. I have been the spender most of my life. I've never been one to feel excited about having a savings account. My mother was a saver, yet we never really discussed money management or budgeting. My father was always the spender. My father and stepmother lived paycheck to paycheck and never prepared for the future.

Along with the two-thirds of Americans who were recently unable to pass a basic financial literacy test, I didn't learn how to manage my money in an appropriate manner when I was young.

I never thought much about something happening or not being able to work right through retirement. I never felt we needed more than a few thousand dollars in savings. I had credit card debt, student loans and car loans.

At my most desperate, I even took out a few payday loans in my early 20s and eventually ended up filing for bankruptcy at the age of 24. Yikes!

Reading Dave Ramsey's book really shifted my perspective. I recognized that a spender mentality doesn't work if you want to have money and a positive net worth.

As a spender, I didn't see that my actions were limiting the amount of money our family was saving for our future. Now, looking back after a change in perspective, I can see that we would be much further ahead in our retirement plans if I'd had restraint and said no to my impulsive spending behaviors. We would have been more prepared to help our children with college tuition. Half of the items I purchased I don't even have anymore. Most have been sold in garage sales or donated.

For what? Instant gratification, feeding a borderline shopping addiction, and trying to fill a void that could never be filled externally.

In an interview about addiction, Russell Brand said everyone that is addicted to anything is trying to feel better or feel good. At first, the object of your addiction does make you feel better. But after the addict consumes his poison, he is left with guilt and remorse. We addicts keep chasing that good feeling. Because we didn't feel safe as children, for whatever reason, we never learned to sit still long enough to find that happiness is within us. We chase happiness, not realizing it is on the other side of the pain and shame we're numbing within ourselves. And because we aren't happy, we keep reaching for something to take the edge off, to give us a momentary sense of relief.

This was exactly how I felt. I went shopping when I was frustrated, overwhelmed or angry. Retail therapy!! We've all heard the term. Our society encourages it. That was my excuse for many years. Purchasing something, anything, made me feel instantly better for a short time.

If you are the spender in your marriage, sit with yourself and figure out why you spend. Again, looking in the mirror isn't always easy. But it can be done. Once I understood the reasons behind my need to shop, I was able to recognize where I could begin to fix myself and change my negative behavior patterns. I saw that consumption wouldn't help me solve any of my problems. In fact, like all addictions, it made my problems and my marriage worse.

This section isn't meant to discuss addiction. It's about figuring out why you do what you do with regards to money. Your reason for being a spender may be different from mine. I've heard some say they spend because they don't believe they will live forever. I am sure you have too. This phrase comes to mind:

"You can't live forever or take it with you when you die."

This is true, and I say go for it if you don't have a spouse or children. But chances are you have one and most likely both, since you are reading this book.

If you have a spouse and children, it's time to listen up!

Have you heard of Murphy's Law? Dave Ramsey talks about it a lot in *The Total Money Makeover*. If you don't have an emergency fund, you need one! I am living proof that an emergency fund is necessary. (I know, I'm living proof of a lot of things!) Why? Because Murphy WILL come calling. Murphy can come in the form of job loss, illness, a broken hot water heater, unexpected hospital visits, home break-ins—I'm sure you can conjure up a few of your own examples. For us, it was MS. In the worst-case scenarios, I've had friends who lost their spouses to accidents, heart attacks and cancer at very young ages.

Here is a thought-provoking question, God forbid you should lose your spouse tomorrow. Would you have enough money to pay for a small funeral? Most people don't. Why do you think we see so many GoFundMe pages requesting assistance in paying funeral expenses? It's actually written in their slogan and is the number two option on their drop-down lists of reasons to start a fundraiser. To have a person's remains cremated costs over $1,000. That fee doesn't include any additional services, just cremation.

Two years ago, a friend of mine lost her husband to a heart attack at age 40. She spent upward of $15,000 for a traditional funeral, with casket, viewing, burial, service, plot and gravestone. That amount doesn't take into account the children left behind to feed, clothe and shelter.

That is a frightening thought if you have nothing saved, isn't it?

Before we had an amount equivalent to more than six months of expenses saved in our emergency fund, it seemed like unexpected expenses popped up regularly. It was so stressful, on many levels. We had to deal with the situation at hand, which is stressful enough in itself. Now tack on a large expense that we couldn't afford to pay with cash (because we didn't have much saved). So, we put it on the credit card, which left us with anywhere between $1,000 and $5,000 in credit card debt accruing 27 percent interest. Now we have locked ourselves into a new monthly payment.

We didn't have much left over after our bills were paid.

I have to say that one of the most important stress-reducing lessons I have learned in my adult life with money is this:

IF I CAN'T PAY CASH, I CAN'T AFFORD IT!

Don't think, "We can afford the payment." Rather, look at

the actual cost of what you are purchasing. Do you have that much cash without digging into your emergency fund? If the answer is no, you cannot afford the purchase. My advice is open a savings account at your local bank and pay yourself the monthly payment you would make, with interest, to the credit card company. Once the money is saved, see if you still desire that item. If the desire is still as strong, make the purchasing decision together, as a couple.

It took a long time and many different money management strategies to get Jason and me on the same page.

It was *The Total Money Makeover* that finally got us there, to a place of peace and comfort with finances in our relationship. We've tried dividing our money and paying our individual expenses separately. We paid based on our income percentages, since he made more money than I did. I learned quickly that this wouldn't work with my spending habits. I racked up more credit card debt and pretended like I had it all figured out financially. We've tried individually taking over the budget and finances and not having a budget at all. None of these scenarios worked well.

When we did decide to recombine our accounts and work together, I kept a secret credit card for about a year. I canceled that card the day my husband came home and described my secret purchases as "financial infidelity." This term hit me like a bullet to the heart. I'd never heard the phrase and it revealed the depth of damage I had created in the financial realm of our relationship.

My spending created a sense of distrust. So, not only did I have to work out why shopping and spending were my addiction and outlet, but I also had to earn my husband's trust back.

It took several years.

We have followed Dave Ramsey to a tee, and over the past few years, we have been able to modify certain aspects to fit our marriage and life specifically. For example, we no longer need to operate on the cash envelope system. Jason has never been a spender and for the past two years, I have adopted the saver's mentality. Neither of us has the urge to spend often. When we do, we discuss pros and cons and make a decision together. We usually end up talking ourselves out of the purchase. For me, it's been a long process to become a saver. I still don't get overly excited about saving. What I do like is the journey in learning patience. I like being able to overcome the initial impulse to buy. I feel like the less I spend, the more money we make.

I also found great insight in *The Millionaire Next Door* by Thomas J. Stanley and William D. Danko. The authors write that most millionaires in the United States are actually everyday people, living in blue-collar working communities, driving a car that is an average of four years old with fewer than 80,000 miles on it. In 2016, Stanley reported that the cars most commonly driven by these millionaires were American-made, which means you won't see them in a Lexus, Mercedes or BMW.

My biggest takeaway from the book was that making more money isn't the solution to increasing our net worth. It is spending less. When you live below your means, you never feel the need to "keep up with the Joneses."

Additionally, the less you spend, the less you pay Uncle Sam. In other words, the more we spend, the more we are charged in taxes. That goes for every single purchase we make. I feel like I have paid one hell of a lot of money in sales taxes since I became a consumer. I don't want to give more than I have to.

Your Three
Transformative
Questions

How would the way you feel right now change if you had the equivalent of six months of expenses saved? (If you do have a savings fund of this nature already, skip to the next question, and congratulations!)

....

....

....

....

....

....

....

....

....

How would your relationship change if money was never an issue?

....

....

....

....

....

....

....

....

....

....

....

....

....

....

What is the one thing you can do, starting now, to make that happen? What is the one thing your partner can do, starting now, to support your vision for your financial future? Remember, working together toward a common vision makes it exponentially more likely you'll achieve that vision.

....

....

....

....

....

....

....

....

....

....

....

....

CHOOSE TO BE SPIRITUAL PARTNERS

I've learned over the past several years that there is a very big difference between being a married couple and being spiritual partners. To me, spiritual partnership stretches beyond a traditional marriage. Anyone can be married! It takes real commitment and dedication to form a spiritual partnership.

I never understood or even heard of spiritual partnership prior to the past year. I always assumed that we just went with the flow and lived by our wedding vows throughout the duration of our marriage. My husband does his job and performs his husbandly duties and I do the same, fulfilling the wife role.

When our children were very little, much of our time together felt like a business relationship. Often, we were ships passing in the night. I worked night shift and he worked day shift. We called this phase "the thick of parenting." All our time and energy was focused on the necessities of the daily grind, keeping these little humans alive while maintaining some form of sanity.

Both of us were sleep deprived and cranky, trying to work outside of the home, keeping up with homework and the life of our older kids via school pick-ups and drop-offs, ushering them to and from sports and friends and attempting to be present for them while waking up to feed and change the baby every two hours.

After the first, that good old tip to rest when your baby is sleeping goes entirely out the window. We go into pure survival mode.

Rather than Jay and I focusing on each other, we were enveloped in what I like to call grenade parenting. For about two years with each child, mindfulness went out the window, as did the nice evening walks to reconnect and and give the support all partners need. There were many days where I couldn't find the time or energy to even take a shower, let alone give my husband my undivided attention to listen to what happened during his day.

I wish someone would have told me that it's normal to feel completely overwhelmed and not be entirely connected to my husband in the thick of parenting kids who were, say, 11, eight, two and six months old.

I thought there was something wrong with me for not being able to maintain a perfectly clean home, have perfectly happy children, work night shifts at the hospital, have a social life with playdates, and still be able to have quality time with my husband at the end of the day. This is the thick of parenting. It will pass. The days seem to drag on during this phase, but the years fly by. Yes, it stinks. But lean in on each other. Love and nourish one another. Do not become each other's punching bags. It will only deplete your energy further. Believe me, it may not be instant or obvious, but what you give out comes back. You set the tone for your relationships, and when you're able to be gentle in the toughest of spots, you're creating a life for yourself that is gentle and forgiving.

The goal is to give yourself and your partner grace, love and forgiveness. We all get tired and we all have too much on our plates at some stage of marriage and parenting.

If you think your partner should do more, wait until you're calm and then sit down and have a respectful conversation about what you need. Remind each other that these few short years will pass more quickly than you believe.

You must find a way to communicate effectively and respectfully, even when you are so sleep deprived that you want to break something because someone didn't pick up their dirty underwear and put them in the hamper.

You and your partner are going to be the only two left standing in your crazy, busy house once your kids are grown. They will eventually want to go out into the world on their own. If you find a way to work as a united front together, tackling life's challenges and obstacles as a team, you allow these challenging times to create a lasting bond of togetherness.

Bestselling author Gary Zukav describes spiritual partnership as a relationship beyond the five senses. Spiritual partnership is paying attention to our actions and taking accountability for them, while supporting the spiritual growth and development of our partner. Ultimately, we want to lift each other up and provide the best environment to foster each other's positive growth. Our partner doesn't need to hold us accountable because when we are in a spiritual partnership, we do this for ourselves.

To me, spiritual partnership is taking off the blinders of tunnel vision and recognizing that our actions have a direct impact on the people around us.

Once I did this, I also chose to think and act in favor of my marriage rather than just for myself or my friends, family members or anyone outside of my marriage. The only opinions that matter are yours and your partner's.

Early on in my marriage to Jason, I was concerned about how people would perceive me and our relationship; I acted accordingly. The problem with this rationale is that a lot of people will overstep their boundaries even if they know you are married or in a relationship.

For example, Jason and I rarely drink alcohol these days, but we both used to drink quite a bit more in social situations, especially if he was out with his friends or I was out with mine. This made us both uncomfortable, and we'd question what went on when we weren't together.

After several nights of too many drinks followed by arguments, we decided that if we drink, we drink together. We both decided that we didn't want to make each other feel like our relationship might be in jeopardy. Most importantly to me, I never wanted Jason to think I don't have our relationship always at the forefront of my mind.

People poke fun at our boundaries, and that is okay. I know others won't necessarily agree with what works for us. I have heard people say that we are both jealous, we don't trust each other, one of us must have done something bad, ol' ball and chain and so on. Those so-called friends are no longer part of our lives.

I am not suggesting that you should have the exact same boundaries that Jason and I do. I am saying that if I do something that makes my spouse feel uncomfortable, I need to recognize it, take accountability for it, and act to change it. This goes back to surrendering to one another.

In any relationship, we want to be loved, desired and cared for—to have a feeling of security and trust. This is a two-way street. You must recognize how your actions affect your partner and care enough to avoid hurting them. You want to ensure you provide a nurturing, loving and safe environment for your partner to grow into their best self.

Spiritual partnership is about loving and caring about your partner, just as you would yourself. This is why the first and most critical step is self-love. If you can fall madly, deeply in love with yourself, free from ego, you can easily share that kind of love with your partner.

It's time to build your partnership up! Build one another. It is time to stop fighting against each other. Spiritual partnership is a deep understanding. It is knowing that this is your person, always there for you, in the good times and bad.

Your Three Transformative Questions

How solid is the trust in your relationship? Given that we all have a trust baseline that is established early in our lives, what is one thing you could do to build trust with your partner? What is one thing he or she could do to build trust with you?

....

....

....

....

....

....

....

....

Is your home a safe and nurturing place for every member of your family? If not, what has to change?

....

....

....

....

....

....

....

....

....

....

....

....

....

....

If trust is an issue in your relationship with your partner, how much of the mistrust between you pertains to your relationship and how much pertains to your personal histories?

....

....

....

....

....

....

....

....

....

....

....

....

....

THE
RIPPLE
EFFECT

I sat in a church pew, dumbfounded, listening to Pastor Scott's sermon. He had confidence that bordered on cocky. With dark, short hair and brown eyes hidden behind thick black frames, he wore jeans and a tight-fitting tee shirt that ensured we all knew he worked out daily. He never had a problem speaking his truth or exposing his vulnerability to the 4,000 or so people who attended our mega-church. He was not your typical pastor. He was in his mid-30s and often spoke of his love for UFC fighting and jujitsu. When he took the stage and spoke about his love for God and his wife and children, you could hear a pin drop. We listened raptly to his teachings on the importance of family and how to have a peaceful, loving marriage in today's world.

On this particular Sunday, he spoke of the ripple effect of our thoughts and actions.

He used an example of a woman getting ready for work in the morning. She goes through her normal routine, fixing her hair and makeup and getting dressed. While she looks in the mirror, she decides to make herself up a bit more than usual, hoping that an attractive coworker might notice her. This wouldn't be a big deal—if she wasn't married to someone else.

It doesn't matter what has been happening in the marriage up to this point. This is an event that will cause a ripple of effects. Whether or not she even speaks a word, the thought is there, and her energy is shifting. Human beings sense the energy shift. Eventually, and whether he is aware of it or not, her spouse will sense this shift also.

Of course, on the surface, we all know this is inappropriate and can lead to consequences that range from nothing more than a thought to an affair and the destruction of a family. Her thought, put into motion, can be catastrophic.

The thought is a potential gateway into more damaging behavior.

Jason always says, "Never do or say anything that you wouldn't do with your partner standing right next to you."

This is so wise and so very important. It isn't about jealousy, but about respecting our relationship and partnership.

It is easy to say. But how many people actually live by this motto? Sadly, I've seen so many relationships sucked down a rabbit hole of infidelity with what started out as an innocent text message. Your thoughts and actions will always have a ripple effect. This effect will cause the ripples to carry on and on, far further than just you and your partner.

As a mother, I've had to answer the questions of my older children about the cause of my divorces from their fathers. In one marriage, I was the adulterer. The ripple effect was certainly not something I was thinking about 18 years ago when I was making impulsive decisions and not taking my child into consideration. I felt bad and I wanted to feel better; it felt so easy and natural to go toward the attention I was receiving from someone new.

It was very difficult to look into my teenage son's eyes and tell him honestly that I made a selfish decision that affected his life so seriously and to sincerely apologize. I'm grateful that my kids are so good at holding me accountable for my actions. It has given me the opportunity to reflect, apologize and help heal their wounds. In turn, it's helped to heal my own.

I was truly oblivious to the respect, compassion, love and grace needed in a marriage. I didn't value the sanctity of marriage. How could I? I knew almost nothing about healthy, stable relationships, let alone joyous ones.

On the opposite side of the relationship spectrum, the ripple effect can do beautiful, wonderful things in your relationship. If you throw a few good rocks into the river of life, those ripples will carry on too, blessing your partner, your children and yourself.

After a few years of being with Jason, I noticed that he never checked out other women, even out of the corner of his eye, when we were together. (I found myself checking out other women and comparing myself to them all the time.) Enveloped in my own insecurity, I watched where Jason's eyes were wandering every time we were out.

Much to my surprise, he never did pay attention to other women and still doesn't to this day. When we were out to dinner with a group of friends, I heard remarks from a few of the husbands and single friends. ("Nice rack." Imaginative.) Without skipping a beat, Jason would reply with a comment like my favorite, "She's not as beautiful as my wife."

Our society has done a very good job of making objectifying behavior acceptable. Personally, I am proud of all the women and men stepping forward in the #MeToo movement. I hope this is the beginning of the end of accepting the sexual objectification of any human being.

The one and only time I thought I caught Jason checking out another woman, we were at the mall, walking through the Gap. An attractive woman in a white top and long wispy skirt strolled by.

I noticed immediately that Jason's eyes shifted toward her; he gazed for less than half a second. Of course, I was ready to pounce on him—I'd been waiting for this since we met. But I was stunned by what came out of his mouth. "Have you ever thought about getting a skirt like that? I think that style would look really great on you."

I was confused. I was at the forefront of his thoughts? This was an important experience and learning lesson for me. It brought me a sense of peace, knowing that my husband desires me and doesn't think of other women in that way.

This is a glimpse into spiritual partnership. This is my person, who protects my heart and soul. He only thinks of me and I of him. We are fully vulnerable to one another. Each ripple of love and positivity draws our hearts closer to one another.

The ripple effect is another way of describing the process of building trust and mutual respect in a marriage or partnership. In Brené Brown's captivating TED Talk, which has been viewed more than eight million times, she describes trust as a jar of marbles. Each action either adds a marble to the jar of trust or it removes one. Trust is not gained through one interaction with another human being. It is gained through a series of actions throughout the duration of each relationship. Many small actions lead to large results over time. It takes time to develop a sense of trust in our relationships. We need to remember that each decision we make will have a result, good or bad.

I've learned through a great deal of trial and error over the years that each marble either placed into or taken out of the relationship trust jar causes a direct ripple of love or of discontent. We won't always make the decision that best suits our partner. We will falter, and we will have tests arise within our relationships.

Life doesn't always go as smoothly and perfectly as I would like. However, if I stick to my intention, I know that my first thought will always be, "How will this decision affect Jason?" Of course, I still make decisions that irritate him from time to time, but he knows that my intention is never to harm him, our relationship, or our family.

This kind of intimacy and trust takes years to build. Conversely, it can take one decision to destroy a lifetime of trust. Jason and I have worked hard over the past 11 years to build this level of trust. I will be damned if I allow one bad decision to alter what we've worked so hard to create.

We collectively protect the house of marriage, built brick by brick, row by row, nail by nail. We have both put our blood, sweat and tears into building this home for ourselves and our children.

Pastor Scott's sermon also taught me not to leave the front

door unlocked. There are greedy people in the world who prey on men and women who seem bored or are unhappy in their marriages. There are also good people who make terrible decisions and allow their impulses and emotions to control their actions.

According to an article published in *Women's Health* magazine, only 60 percent of married women report being happy in their marriages. Additionally, a 2009 Gallup poll found that two-thirds of Americans filing for divorce are women.

I have been among them. I filed for two out of my three divorces, citing irreconcilable differences. I have been desperate for someone, anyone, to treat me like an attractive human being. While I didn't actively pursue other people, I certainly didn't have my guard up. I wasn't defending or protecting my marriage.

When Jason and I decided to put our marriage above all else, we both made the commitment to defend it. We are very strict about the boundaries of our marriage because I never want to make him feel that he needs to question my intentions. He wants me to know, without question, of his loyalty to me and our family.

Pastor Scott said it very well when he talked about how we should defend our home from robbers, thieves, snakes and manipulators. He said, "I don't ride in a car alone with another woman." He continued, "I know what I am capable of, as a human being." He said that the love he has for his wife is so important that he would never allow himself to be put in a situation where a destructive thought could enter his mind.

When I first heard that, I thought it was a bit out there. It's no big deal to ride in a vehicle with someone of the opposite sex. But as time went on, that sermon stayed with me and began to resonate. If I never rode alone with a man other than Jason, then he would never have the questions the ego mind seems to weave through relationships.

If we had full and complete trust in our partner, there would be no such thing as jealousy. In my moment of clarity, I recognized that I had never even considered how that could make Jason feel. I began to recognize that part of his defenses in protecting our home was that he never looked at other women. It was such a simple thing to do, in his mind. We really hadn't ever discussed it and he didn't know how much that single decision filled our trust jar over the years.

Both partners should choose to defend the marriage, the home you've built. Don't relax and leave the doors unlocked while you sleep. Protect it! Keep the doors locked at night and pay attention to what you allow in. Here's the thing: if Jason told me that I was never to ride alone in a vehicle with another man, I would feel that he doesn't have faith in me or see me as a capable adult. But if I tell Jason I've decided not to ride alone in a car with another man that isn't a family member, it is my gift to him. I am not saying get crazy with restrictions on one another—I'm pretty sure that will work in the opposite way to what you intend. I am saying that when you surrender to each other and decide what your boundaries will be and then stick to them, your relationship will be enriched. Your marriage is *sacred*. Hold yourself accountable! But ... don't forget grace and forgiveness. This is a process.

Some boundaries we've established in our marriage won't necessarily work for you. As I stated early in the book, I know marriage isn't "one size fits all." Establishing relationship boundaries needs to be a joint effort. (And it really doesn't matter what I, your brother-in-law or Joe at work thinks.) Talk to each other about what makes you feel vulnerable or fearful. Let your partner know what actions put you on the defensive or trigger you. Discuss ways in which you can both compromise to reduce the frequency of triggering. Now, this doesn't mean that you are responsible for healing your partner's wounds. Even if you wanted to, you couldn't do so without their deeply committed cooperation. But you can work together to make your relationship a safe place to do that essential work and grow together.

Jason and I are often called old-fashioned, probably because of our boundaries, which we've tailored together, specifically for our marriage. We choose to live this way out of respect and love for one another, not out of force, suppression, coercion or manipulation. We established these boundaries because we have been faced with scenarios that negatively affected our relationship. We talked about it, found solutions to the issues, and changed our behavior.

Here are some of the boundaries that work for us:

- ⇒ We aren't friends with and don't communicate with people who attempt to bring any sort of drama into our relationship or cross into the gray area of flirtation.
- ⇒ We don't go out with single friends on a regular basis.
- ⇒ We usually go out together.
- ⇒ We are never alone with someone of the opposite sex.
- ⇒ We aren't friends with many people of the opposite sex individually.
- ⇒ We talk about each other positively to our friends and other people we encounter.

⇒ We keep our challenges private and work them out together, most of the time.

⇒ I choose to wear a more modest wardrobe. I'm not talking long skirts and shirts with long sleeves. (Hey, if that is for you, I am not judging.) But I do dress in a way that is comfortable for me and for Jason. I don't like to draw the attention of other men. Again, this is just what works for us.

I have several friends who have a boundary of not associating with ex-lovers. My stepfather, on the other hand, used to be very good friends with his ex-wife and she and my mom got along well.

I have a very beautiful friend and her husband likes it when she dresses in sexier clothing when they are out with friends or on a date night. She feels confident and sexy in what she wears, while he loves seeing her flaunt what her mama gave her. That is what works for them.

Go on and choose your boundaries together. Write out a list of what is most important to you and ask your partner to do the same. Don't let it become a he said, she said. It's not a negotiation. This is allowing yourselves to be real and vulnerable with each other. Listen to what your partner says. Try on your empathy hat and ask that they do the same. Set some boundaries that align with your shared intentions for your relationship. Then, the actions: do your best to stick to those intentions and honor those boundaries.

I promise you that you won't regret it.

Your Three Transformative Questions

What boundary are you comfortable setting for yourself today that could help safeguard your relationship in the future?

....

....

....

....

....

....

....

....

....

....

What is a boundary that comes to mind for you right now that your partner could set that would make you feel safer and cherished? What is a boundary that comes to mind right now that you could set to make your partner feel safer and cherished?

....

....

....

....

....

....

....

....

....

....

....

....

Is there anything you do that you wouldn't do if your partner
was standing beside you? If so, are you willing to stop?

....

....

....

....

....

....

....

....

....

....

....

....

....

....

LOYALTY IS EARNED THROUGH ACTION

In preparation for this book, I polled many men and women in our community—married, divorced, widowed, remarried, high school sweethearts, late bloomers, single, gay, straight, open relationships, Evangelical, Catholic, Mormon, agnostic, spiritualists and regular Joes. I asked the following question:

What is the most important aspect of your marriage?

The most common answer from this large, diverse group of people? Loyalty! (Quick shout out to those of you who participated! Thank you!)

Before we can really delve into growing or earning loyalty in your relationship, we should probably define it. According to Webster's, loyalty is:

1. the quality of being loyal to someone or something.
2. a strong feeling of support or allegiance.

A strong feeling of support or allegiance. Let this sink in. Who do you feel is your greatest ally? Your ride or die? The peanut butter to your jam? Who stands by you in the best of times and the worst of times? Who picks you up from the floor when you need lifting? Is this your spouse? Is this your partner?

If you choose to be spiritual partners, you are loyal to your partner first and foremost. It does not matter what others think, say, feel or do or don't do. It needs to be the two of you first, every time!

Every step, rule, task and offering we have talked about to this point leads to loyalty. If you are kind, loving and forgiving of yourself, you will begin to define the boundaries of what you are willing to accept in your life, your relationships and marriage.

We are an alliance, working together—if we have each other's backs, it means everything is easier. We can take on more, succeed more, make our dreams come true more. I know Jason will be there for me when I need the extra help. I know he won't throw me under the bus with his friends when I have had a rough day and thoughtlessly snapped at him. (He knows that when I have a rough day and thoughtlessly snap at him, I'll apologize and try to make it up to him.) I know that he will love me and support me, just as I will be there for him.

Never attacking me, being present in our conversations even when I am venting, listening without judgment, standing by my side, being supportive of my feelings—it all seems so simple, yet it is the raw material of loyalty. Each moment strengthens my faith in his loyalty to me, and my loyalty to him deepens even further.

It would be so easy to turn our personal frustrations on each other and begin nitpicking at little things. But we choose to be there and support each other rather than to be each other's punching bag.

Loyalty is very much like the marbles in the jar we discussed in the previous chapter. The more trust you have in your partner and your relationship, the stronger your alliance is. The stronger your alliance, the better security system you have in place to protect your marriage.

Loyalty forms a web of connectedness that becomes difficult for anyone, anything or any situation to penetrate.

If you want more loyalty, start with small marbles of trust. Have your partner's best interest at the forefront of your thoughts. Have the positive intention to put your relationship and spouse above all else. Love and forgive. Choose to see the beauty and point it out.

We all want to be loved and accepted. Time, positive intention, love and always having your partner's back create unshakeable loyalty—and loyalty makes life better.

Your Three Transformative Questions

What does loyalty mean to you?

....

....

....

....

....

....

....

....

....

....

Do you feel that your partner is loyal to you? Why or why not? If not, what has to change?

....

....

....

....

....

....

....

....

....

....

....

....

....

....

Do you feel that you are loyal to your partner? Why or why not? If not, what has to change?

....

....

....

....

....

....

....

....

....

....

....

....

....

....

LEARN HOW TO LISTEN TO EACH OTHER

One of the top challenges in relationships is communication between partners.

We are so impressionable when we are young children, and our first lessons in communication happen when we watch our parents or caregivers. If you were raised in a "kids need to keep quiet until spoken to" family, like I was, you might internalize your thoughts and feelings, leading to discord within yourself. If you were raised in a household of screamers, chances are you are a screamer when your emotions take over.

My stepmother was a big-time screamer and fit-thrower. She screamed, yelled, kicked, broke stuff, hit, punched and threw whatever she could. She had incredible fits of rage that would often last for several days at a time. My mom, on the other hand, wasn't a screamer until I pushed her to her breaking point. That seemed to be the way I could make her really pay attention to me, especially in my teenage years.

I regularly heard my father and stepmother tell one another to "fuck OFF!" They used horrible, offensive, below-the-belt fighting tactics that I now know are detrimental to any relationship. Conflicts got physical.

You can probably guess this did not result in a successful, happy, healthy and thriving relationship.

The point is, we all come from very different backgrounds. And for the most part, we practice what we have learned from our parents. A corollary of this is that our parents' behavior sets our benchmark: if our parents were physically abusive, and we only abuse our kids and spouse emotionally, we can feel like we're doing pretty good. If our parents were emotionally abusive and we simply withdraw and are absent a lot of the time, we can tell ourselves we're okay.

After my failed marriages, I knew I needed to learn how to communicate effectively. I had taken all the clinical psychology and psychiatry requirements and clinicals during college and nursing school, so I knew the basics of effective therapeutic communication with my patients.

Yet I never learned how to communicate when I was triggered. Once my amygdala took over, I was hijacked by a fit of rage. Screaming obscenities, using words that cut like a knife, arguing to the point of exhaustion. Minus the physical abuse, I acted like my stepmother at her very worst, not someone I wanted to emulate.

Jason and I had one year of ineffective communication. At our lowest of lows, I learned so much. I learned about his triggers and weak spots. I also learned that I never again want to return to that space. I never want to be the cause of that pain. In that darkness, I learned a very valuable lesson about respecting him and never using his vulnerabilities against him.

In that moment, I was clear that verbally hitting below the belt was off limits forevermore.

We sat down together, discussed our triggers and set our intention to help raise each other to the next level of thinking rather than pulling each other into an ugly spiral of blaming and accusing.

I've learned that if I start to become angry and raise my voice, I can step away for five minutes, separate myself from my amygdala's primal reaction to fight or run, and remember that I am not the emotion I am feeling. As Eckhart Tolle states in his book *A New Earth*, I am the observer of my reactions and emotions. My reactions and emotions are not me; neither do they control me.

Of course, therapeutic communication is great for not making your partner feel attacked when you are upset about something. But before we get to this point, you need to look inward. (I know ... AGAIN?!) Why is this situation so upsetting to you? If it is something that needs addressing, wait until you're calm and then approach your spouse with care and compassion. Don't attack. Explain your position. We don't have to always be right or have the last word. Be willing to close your mouth and listen empathetically to your partner's interpretation and intention. Hold yourself accountable for any part you've played in the situation and talk peacefully, kindly and lovingly. Don't let your spouse be the scapegoat or punching bag for your irritability. This is your person—the last person you should attack.

Ego cannot run the show when communicating with your spouse. If someone loves you and you love them enough to spend the rest of your lives together, he or she should always be spoken to from a place of love.

Notice I say love, not enablement. There is no love without respect, and there is no respect that doesn't recognize a person's ability and responsibility to be accountable. But allowing someone to be accountable is the opposite of shaming and blaming—it is saying, calmly and with unconditional love, "I know you aim higher. I know how hard you try. You'll do better the next time, I know you will."

THE EGO BEACH

When you listen to the inner dialogue of your ego, you'll find it is always in the mode of save and protect. Before we can go further with communication, I would like to take some time to delve into ego specifically.

What is ego? Before I began studying spirituality and mediumship, I never really had a definition. I would have said ego is the way a person thinks they are better than the rest of the world. I equated ego with narcissism. This is partially true.

Webster's dictionary defines ego as: a person's sense of self-esteem or self-importance.

Throughout my mediumship training, we've done a lot of exercises on recognizing where self-dialogue originates in the mind and the types of communication we receive, as well as how to address learning and redevelop previously ingrained neuropathways.

Here is another way to look at it. We all have an inner dialogue. Remember the angel on one shoulder and the little devil on the other from cartoons as a kid? This is basically bringing to life the inner voices that make up the nonstop dialogue you have with yourself daily. To me, ego is the little devil and my higher self is the angel. Ego is fear-driven; my higher self is love-driven.

Pay attention to how you talk to yourself. When you are down on yourself, where does this inner dialogue come from? Which part of your head?

For me, my ego dialogue comes from the left side of my head, just behind my left ear. The dialogue is worry, guilt, shame, fear, anger, frustration and self-loathing. My positive inner dialogue comes in on the right side of my head, right above my right eye, in my frontal lobe region. This is the motivator voice: positive, calming, effective and solution-driven.

When you can recognize where your thoughts are coming from and the type of conversation each part of your mind is formulating for you, you can take back your power from your emotions and thoughts. You recognize that you get to control which inner dialogue you choose to flood your mind with. (I can assure you that any fear you have regarding your relationship is coming from ego.)

In the 18-week mediumship certification course I took with my beautiful mentors Lillian and Lou Ann, we learned to differentiate the dialogue, locate the origination and name our ego and higher self. The reason for this lesson is to honor the ego rather than shame and disregard it.

When my ego starts to take over, I find it helpful to stop and recognize where the thoughts are coming from. When the source is my ego, I thank it for trying to protect me from danger. I assure my ego that its protection is not necessary. I thank it for all the times it protected me before I had self-love to do that job.

With this awareness, I have chosen not to see my ego as something I need to fight, but something that protected me when I lived in a difficult world surrounded by difficult people. My ego gives me a run for my money pretty much every day. When I begin to get nervous over a reading or writing this book or communication with a person who makes me uncomfortable, my ego starts an inner dialogue that goes something like this:

"I am going to fail at this. I might as well not even try. Why keep going? It's all just overwhelming. What if I fail? What if people don't like what I am creating?"

I stop the dialogue as soon as I recognize that it's occurring. I thank my ego for trying to protect me. I tell her, "You have worked so hard protecting me all of these years. You have done your job and I appreciate all of your hard work. Please feel free to sit back and relax now. You get to retire. My higher self is fresh and ready to take the wheel of my thoughts and life."

Yep, pretty much every day I tell my ego this. Rather than having an argument between the angel and devil on my shoulder, I essentially am giving the devil on my shoulder a mai tai and a beach to relax on. My ego is much like a teenager. If you think about it, most egos are very teen-like. The ego sees things from a one-person perspective. It fills in the gaps in any story without any proof. It is absolutely sure it is right, and any evidence to the contrary is seen as a threat.

Needless to say, this can be very damaging in any relationship.

We have all fallen victim to filling in the gaps. Jason used to play poker on Wednesday nights with friends. I knew where he was going to be and what time he would be home. He would call on breaks to let me know how he was doing in the tournament, and then go back to playing. Now, throw in a hypothetical scenario. Jason goes to play poker and I don't hear from him after the first hour of the tournament. Early in our relationship, my ego would start to question the situation. I might ask myself, "Where is he?" "Why isn't he calling?" "Is he out with another woman?" "Oh my God, was he in an accident?" My ego creates a whole mess of problems for me to worry about in less than a second.

When he gets home, how is my mood? After thinking up all these horrible scenarios and playing them out in my mind, I am angry that he didn't think of me, didn't understand how I'd worry.

In actuality, his phone died, and he didn't have a charger. It was not a big deal.

Ego automatically goes to worst-case scenarios. This has been in our DNA since the beginning of human existence. It's a defense mechanism that has protected our survival for thousands of years.

Ego takes us directly to fight, flight or freeze after it mindfucks us into submission. The submission is a way to get us to stand still, never push through comfort, and never get hurt. Ego tries to keep us safe, but it is not optimized for happiness.

The ego isn't something we need to fight. It is a part of who we are. It is a piece of our darkness, which is necessary to balance our light. Our ego is not our enemy. If we treat it as such, we will not subdue it. Rather, we will fuel it.

When we allow our higher selves to take over our thoughts and perceptions, interactions and daily life, the darkness begins to fade and the light and beauty in the world around us begins to make itself more apparent. We realize that everything isn't a direct attack on us. We can problem solve. We see through the eyes of love.

I highly recommend that you begin practicing this daily. As soon as you recognize that you are having the inner dialogue, stop. Step into the perspective of the observer. What is the feeling of your inner dialogue? What is your mind saying to you? Where is it coming from?

Once you can recognize that you are not your thoughts or actions, you have the power to transcend the ego. As Eckhart Tolle writes, you cannot be the emotion or thought, because you can recognize that you are having the thought. So, the thought isn't you. You are the observer, observing the world you have attracted and are cocreating with God/Universe/Source.

When you recognize that ego is taking the wheel of your life, you have the choice to allow your higher self to come forward and take over. In a marriage, when both of you come from that higher-self place of love, you can begin to move mountains together. Then the communication begins to flow!

Jason and I have figured out over the years that sometimes communicating effectively is just staying quiet. Let me explain what I mean.

We all have stressful days and days when we are cranky or short with each other and the world around us. Every person is battling something. Every person has challenges they are working through, whatever their age, race, gender, religion and social status. Feeling the energy of your partner and finding compassion and grace when they are not at their best is so important.

Pay attention to the feeling when your partner walks into the room. Is it stress? Is it gratitude? Is it love? Is it irritation? Is it anger? Is it depression? Feelings speak.

When I am having a challenging day and my patience is stretched thin, I do tend to spout off a smart-ass comment from time to time. I do get frustrated when I see the trash can is full and every other human being in the house continues to re-create the Leaning Tower of Pisa by piling more trash atop. Three, four, five times I walk by the dreaded trash can and the pile just keeps getting larger. I want to scream, "Does anyone else care about the fact that the trash is overflowing?? Oh, no worries!! Mom will take care of it, as always!"

Obviously, not my best me. But if I am going to be completely honest, I do have a temper and I do get frustrated. I also do tend to globalize in my moments of frustration, as in using the words always and never. If you feel this way, you are not alone. I've learned that when I get into these moods, Jason tends to keep his bottom and top lips touching. Get it? Keeping his mouth shut. But he doesn't keep his mouth shut in submission—he stays quiet because it works. He doesn't provoke me, because fighting ugly with ugly doesn't work, as discussed previously. Even more importantly, I recognize his silence and it snaps me back into my prefrontal cortex. Once I recognize that he isn't engaging in my mood, I am stopped in my tracks pretty much every time. Then I must take accountability for my behavior, apologize for acting like a weeny whiner, take the damn trash out because it really isn't that big of a deal in the grand scheme of life, and change my behavior and my attitude.

To my credit, I have learned and am attempting to master this myself. It's truly amazing what can happen when you don't engage in the argument or the irritation your spouse is displaying. Simply remaining patient, giving your partner grace and loving them despite their current mood changes everything.

I love recognizing this in myself and I love when I recognize this in Jason. We aren't rude with each other; we don't make comments under our breath at one another. We just exist in the space and we support one another through the moment's struggle. Within 15 minutes, we almost always feel grateful that we allowed each other to feel how we felt, without taking it personally, feeling attacked and attacking back. (When you recognize your partner is doing this for you, acknowledge and thank them!)

We have had situations where, in the cranky moods, we piss each other off. By remaining quiet during the irritation, you put yourself in observer mode and step away from the emotions.

We have had many times where, a few hours after the incident, Jason will tell me, "Hey, that thing you said when you were cranky did frustrate me." At that point, I need to be empathetic to him and his needs.

I learned another way to manage negative feelings from a very dear friend of mine who happens to be a clinical psychiatric nurse practitioner. She explained this approach to help my children learn to work with their feelings, and I won't lie—when I tried this with my youngest and it snapped him out of a tantrum, I was hooked. I had to try it for myself.

When I begin to feel the stress, anxiety and anger boil up within, I take a moment to stop and recognize where I feel these feelings inside of my body. Personally, I feel most frustration and anger either between my throat and heart or in the pit of my stomach, also known as the solar plexus. I take a few minutes to focus on the feeling and the location. Then I begin to feed into the feeling by concentrating on the pain of the feeling. I push into it. So many of us resist pain. We try to push it away, run from it or avoid it all together—and the result is that we just get stuck in those feelings, or they keep coming up again and again.

Next, I imagine this feeling as a ball of matter, and I hold it out in front of me. I begin to analyze it. Does it hurt? Is it hard or soft? Does it have a shape? Color? Size? Is it dense or easy to penetrate? Can I move it or shape it into something else?

This exercise teaches us that we don't have to fear, resist or run away from our feelings. It gets us in touch with our body and how we react to certain experiences. We learn that we can control the impulses of emotions.

The additional benefit to this exercise is that, by analyzing the feeling, you are pulled from your amygdala back into your higher-level thinking and problem-solving brain.

Here is the step-by-step process:

1. I recognize that I am having a negative thought, feeling or reaction. (For example, I am angry with my husband for not picking up after himself.)
2. I stop the thoughts in my brain to slow the momentum of the negative energy that is flowing into me.
3. I explore where these feelings are affecting my body. Where do I feel the discomfort or pain from the emotion?
4. I inspect the feeling and ask myself these questions:
   → What does this feel like?
   → What does this look like?

➤ Is it soft or hard?
➤ Does it have a color?
➤ Does it have a shape?
➤ Does it have sharp edges or soft edges?
➤ Can I move or manipulate it?
➤ If I focus my energy, can I soften it?
➤ Can I move it out of me and hold it in front of me?

Notice that I am not trying to make the feeling go away or shove it down and hope it will not resurface. The purpose is to acknowledge that the feeling exists. Once we acknowledge and shine the light of our attention on the feeling, we can then accept it. The initial impulse, to react, seems to fade away.

There is no need to judge yourself for your feelings or judge anyone else for making you feel this way. Don't judge yourself when you don't do things exactly correctly. Don't judge your spouse. Try to learn these techniques together.

Another very important lesson to learn within communication with others is to release expectations. No other person in this entire world of almost eight billion people will perceive any given situation in the same manner you do. You may have many beliefs in common, yet no situation will be taken in exactly the same way. So, respect the fact that your partner might interpret any given situation entirely differently. They have their own rationale.

Feelings and emotions are a part of our makeup of environment, upbringing, experiences and what we are taught, along with the genetic factors sprinkled into the mix. How does our brain interpret and process emotion and how does it affect our physical body?

In our normal lives, the vast majority of people wake up to an alarm, get ready for our day, go to work, work all day, come home, prepare dinner, get ready for bed, watch a little television, and finally drift off to sleep in our warm bed, with a roof over our head and locks on the door. We have our food in the refrigerator and freezer, and we have heat and air conditioning to feel comfortable whatever our climate.

There isn't much need for our life-or-death primal, instinctive reactions the vast majority of the time. But our brains haven't evolved as quickly as our society.

As we've covered, our brains evolved to protect us. When our amygdala detects a threat, it goes to work, and our prefrontal cortex goes offline. It doesn't take thought to activate the amygdala, just a sense of threat. The more unsafe we perceived our childhood environment to be, the higher the alert level. In our normal daily lives, the threat may be a rude person on the road, an interaction with an angry person at work, or someone who cuts in front of you in line at Starbucks.

It doesn't take any action on our part to activate the amygdala, but it does take work and self-control to shift from the amygdala and reactivate the prefrontal cortex, the thinking part of our brain.

When I get into this space where I am angry or upset, I tell myself, "This is a learning lesson and it is painful. So, let's learn the lesson!!!" I don't want to be presented with it again.

I am not suggesting that once you start putting the tips and tools in this book into practice, nothing bad will ever happen. We are humans and we are here to grow, learn and love. Most of us are not designed to move forward when we're comfortable. We sit and we don't grow. No matter what your age, you can always learn more about other people and the world around you. We are all going to be faced with challenges and difficulty in our lives. It doesn't matter what age, race, culture, ethnicity or social status we claim. We might be a convicted felon or Mother Teresa. We all have shit going on and stuff we need to overcome.

As I write this book, I am faced with many challenges of daily life and people that I don't have any control over, just like every other person on the planet. I go into slumps of frustration, fear and anger too. I must consciously remember to use the tools that I've learned over the years. I still have the old neuropathways, and sometimes I jump into my old way of thinking without realizing it. It takes time, commitment and the desire to want to change the negativity and become the light more often.

The last bit of communication practice I would like to share is this:

Listen with the intention of hearing your partner. Don't listen with the intention of responding. When you are planning or chomping on your response while your partner is expressing his feelings or concerns, you are not actually listening and taking in his point of view. You may not always agree with his words. But if you want the dignity of your partner listening to you, you need to do it too.

Your Three Transformative Questions

Are you willing to sit with your negative emotion until you become calm again, without acting or speaking?

....

....

....

....

....

....

....

....

....

....

Can you imagine responding with love and understanding to your partner when they are angry?

....

....

....

....

....

....

....

....

....

....

....

....

....

....

When you are hurt by something your partner has done or that you believe he or she has done, are you willing to ask for his or her help to heal? The Buddhist monk Thich Nhat Hanh suggests we put it this way: "Darling, I am suffering. Please help."

....

....

....

....

....

....

....

....

....

....

....

in closing

If you are in a shit marriage and you see no end to your misery, by all means, go and live your life the way you feel is right. I know that each of my marriages has been a huge lesson in learning about myself, what I am willing to endure, heartbreak, learning to love once again, and leaving my baggage at the door. I have learned a lot of very hard yet valuable lessons within each failed marriage. Many were extremely painful and haunted me for the greater part of my adult life. Who am I to tell you what you should and should not do in your marriage or life? I am just another human being with my own perceptions, opinions and beliefs.

Each lesson I have experienced along the way has brought me to right where I sit today. These experiences have shaped and molded me.

I can also tell you that growing through those very difficult times has led me to a place of beauty, contentment and joy I didn't know existed a decade ago. I have learned to accept my husband just as he is. I have been able to experience him helping to lift me up to be a better person, and I feel I have helped to lift him up by loving and supporting him and giving him grace.

The truth is that marriage isn't easy. It's like a roller coaster. It has beautifully high and amazing times with glorious views of the Earth below. It also has very low moments, where it's dark, where we see no light at the end of the tunnel. At times we feel we are chugging along slowly and climbing inch by inch. Other days we feel like we are flying through the days and months. Sometimes when we are flying, we are fearful and hold on for dear life, or we resist and scream or cry. We also have times when we are flying when we put our hands up and laugh until our bellies hurt. Sometimes it is anguish and sometimes it's euphoria. All these situations and times should be yours, together, as a united partnership. Don't resist your partner. Do marriage and this relationship together. Hold onto one another for dear life. Remember the vows you took before God, your friends and family. Standing there, looking into each other's eyes.

Throughout the pages of this book, I've shared with you some of my most beautiful moments within my marriage and I have shared with you some dark days and vulnerable experiences. I do get asked if I regret being married so many times. I feel that that question has layers, some that I have conquered and some that I must keep working through. I can still feel that twinge in my solar plexus that tells me I have not let go entirely; I must tread lightly until I can work through it in a healthy manner when my higher self feels my mind and feelings are ready to release.

I don't regret my experiences, because they have taught me valuable lessons that make up the person I am today. Without those experiences, I would not have gained the understanding discussed in these pages, let alone learned to build the marriage that Jason and I have today.

I don't think regret is the correct word. I don't regret. But I do find myself looking back at some of the things I have done or experiences where I could have spared my children or husband discomfort, when I caused pain to others. Sometimes it is sad for me to think about why I made some of the decisions I did. My intentions were not always pure. I think I was fighting for survival in a dark world. I made choices to bring life into tumultuous times and I feel a sense of guilt for not providing a cushion of security, consistency and most of all stability for my older boys early in their lives. I didn't know it existed, let alone how to achieve a beautiful and loving marriage.

I've had these conversations with my older boys since I began realizing that I needed to own my decisions as a person, mother and wife. We have healed over the years and I recognize that our situations and experiences are part of our journey. So, no. I don't regret being married so many times.

I do, however, regret changing my name so many times!! Ever purchased a home? Well, at the very end of the paperwork process you have to sign your signature. Each and every signature you have ever had, under each name. So, I started with my maiden name. Three signatures there: Danielle Hannan, Danielle Hope Hannan, Danielle H. Hannan. Now, tack on four name changes. I seriously had four pages of signatures! That was embarrassing.

I regret spending so much money on weddings and lawyers. I feel sad that my older children had to come from a broken home. They have had to endure things in their upbringing that children from non-divorced families don't. But I can now look back and see that each of my failed relationships might not have actually been a failure.

Maybe they were successes. Because I was able to learn from each experience. I have been able to better myself, to learn to fully invest in my husband, to build a beautiful home on a beautiful foundation. I've learned not to give up and walk away. I have learned to accept my moments, right where we are, even when we are right in the middle of the bullshit storm. I have learned a great deal about integrity and unconditional love. I am not standing by my man (thank you, Patsy Cline) because I must. I am standing by my man because there is nothing in the world I would rather do.

We have obstacles put in place by our guardian angels, God, The Universe, Spirit, call it what you will. We have these roadblocks where situations must end. People abruptly leave our lives, or we come to a road closed sign.

If things were always perfect and wonderful, we would never move. Sometimes these roadblocks show us that the way we are currently operating isn't effective and we need to change something in ourselves. We may not have created the entirety of issues in our life and marriage, but it is our job to fix ourselves.

I once read that if you can see the lesson from a painful experience, it is then you are healed. I believe this to be true. However, I also believe that in order to grow from the experience, you not only have to see the lesson but learn from it. You have to change what it is that you've been doing. Something you have been doing has brought you to this point where you observe, "Oh! I see what I could have done differently." Now you do it differently and you are free.

I've also heard that if you can talk or write about an experience and it no longer makes you cry, you are healed. Writing this book has been a chapter in my healing and accepting myself on an even deeper level. I feel sad for the girl I once was. I see where I allowed situations to dim my light. I see myself down in the trenches, clawing my way through life, feeling like I was being sucked into a black abyss. I see myself making poor choices, doing misguided things I thought would make me happy.

I see now how much I have grown, and I am proud of the person I have become. I've learned many lessons the hard way. I could never just take the advice of well-meaning people in my life. I am proud to teach my children that we can learn and grow from our mistakes. I am also teaching my children the most valuable lesson of all—to love themselves!

I know that awakening spiritually is seeing my growth and feeling sadness for who I used to be when my ego ran my life. Yes, all that is still a part of me. I feel sad for the hurt and grief I caused others.

I also feel so blessed and grateful that I saw I wasn't operating at my best, that I took the initiative to learn and apply better tools for success in marriage.

I still have people look strangely at me when I tell them Jason and I don't drink alcohol without one another, or I don't put myself in situations to be alone with other men. I used to care what my friends thought. Now, I only care what my husband thinks. And I know he only cares about what I think. Occasionally, situations arise that are out of our control. But because we have built such trust with one another by putting our marriage ahead of everything else, there are no egoic thoughts, jealousy or judgments.

Our beliefs and boundaries are well-defined and clear. When we decided this was how we were going to live to protect our marriage, it wasn't easy. We took a lot of grief from other people. I am a fixer and a people pleaser. It took strength to stand in my marriage beliefs rather than allow the opinions of others to influence me.

Now, the fabulous news. As the years have passed, it's become easy. It's our habit. All the people in my life—some very beautiful friends who have been with me on my entire life journey, some picked up along the way at various stages, and some relatively new—all know and respect how much Jason and I value our marriage. We have a community that respects our boundaries, appreciates what we have built and respects our union.

We had to sacrifice caring about the judgments of others. We had to sacrifice being the norm—there are more unhappy marriages than happy ones. We had to sacrifice friendships. We had to sacrifice ego.

Listing these "sacrifices" now almost seems laughable. But when we were in the thick of shifting our marriage and ridding ourselves of the things that were pulling us down, it was difficult. I cared so much what people thought of me for so long that it took a lot of practice. It required reminding myself why I was going to stand in my power and speak my truth about what was important for my marriage.

If you really, really love your partner and they really, really love you, you discover your truth together. You live it with every thought, every breath, every moment of your life. That is the only "sacrifice" you must make to have a beautiful, loving and growing marriage in which you lift each other up.

The truth is, we all have a past. I am so fortunate that Jason ever so lovingly stepped into the chaos of my life, chose me and developed awesome relationships with my boys. He has carried us and been my rock when I felt I was crumbling. He continues to work hard and provide for our family. Even in the face of life-altering jolts, he stands strong, with unshakable faith. I have grown into a much better person because of his love and grace.

His love has taught me that love is beautiful and not full of hurt and turmoil. I am a good mother, wife and person because we encourage each other to be the best we can.

I was a very broken person when Jason entered my world, yet he has never made me feel embarrassed for my past. He saw right through my mess and dysfunction. He saw the me I didn't know existed. He remained patient and loving while I uncovered and rediscovered the essence of myself.

Today I can encourage you to help each other every single step of the way, knowing that it will bring you long-lasting love, joy and contentment. Take on more some days and allow your partner to take on more when you cannot. Always step together and love one another for who you are, right now. Hold yourself accountable.

ABOVE ALL, GIVE EACH OTHER GRACE.

You'll find that the whole universe acts to lift you up when you do.

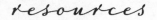
resources

FOR ANYONE
EXPERIENCING ABUSE

If you or someone else is in immediate danger of being
physically harmed, call the emergency services number
in your area.

Otherwise, in the U.S., visit:
womenshealth.gov/relationships-and-safety/get-help
or call the Office of Women's Health (OWN) HELPLINE:
1-800-994-9662 9 a.m. — 6 p.m. ET, Monday-Friday.

In Canada, visit:
justice.gc.ca and search for "get help with family violence."

MORE INFORMATION ON
OTHER TOPICS MENTIONED
IN 4TH TIME'S A CHARM

→ For those experience body image issues, eating disorders and body dysmorphia disorders, visit **psychiatry.org/ patients-families/eating-disorders**. On Instagram, check out former eating disorder sufferer **@bodyposipanda**, yoga teacher **@mynameisjessamyn** and nutritionist **@dietitiancorinne**.

→ For more information on the healing power of gratitude practices, visit the Yale Center for Emotional Intelligence at **ei.yale.edu/what-is-gratitude**. Consider reading the late, great Oliver Sachs' essay "Gratitude" in the New York Times, written just before his death.

→ For more information on the healing power of positive feedback in relationships, start with "What Shamu Taught Me About a Happy Marriage" by Amy Sutherland and then move on to "The Magic Relationship Ratio According to Science" at the Gottman Institute at **gottman.com**.

→ For more strategies for managing flooding or triggers in intimate relationships, read and practice "Making Sure Emotional Flooding Doesn't Capsize Your Relationship" at the Gottman Institute at Gottman.com.

→ For more information on the Adverse Childhood Experiences Study, search for "CDC-Kaiser ACE Study" at the Centers for Disease Control website at **cdc.gov**.

→ For more information on healing from trauma, consider reading psychiatrist Judith Herman's seminal book *Trauma and Recovery*. It's heavy, and deep, but it provides an astonishingly broad, insightful and compassionate study of trauma in modern life.

→ For more information on effective communication during difficult times, google non-violent communication and Marshall Rosenberg for many hours of YouTube lessons that will serve you well. Rosenberg's approach is based on his belief that our language evolved for hierarchical, warring societies and no longer serves us. His framework will give you the confidence to have difficult conversations in loving ways.

TRANSFORMATIVE BOOKS MENTIONED IN 4ᵀᴴ TIME'S A CHARM

→ **On marriage:**
The Love Dare by Stephen Kendrick and Alex Kendrick

→ **On trauma:**
Waking the Tiger—Healing Trauma by Peter Levine

→ **On money:**
The Total Money Makeover by Dave Ramsey

→ **On effective communication:**
Living Nonviolent Communication: Practical Tools to Connect and Communicate Skillfully in Every Situation by Marshall Rosenberg

→ **On self-love and emotional intelligence:**
Love Yourself Like Your Life Depends on It by Kamal Ravikant
Dying to Be Me by Anita Moorjani
Choose Yourself by James Altucher
Judgment Detox by Gabrielle Bernstein
The Power of Now by Eckhart Tolle

Seat of the Soul by Gary Zukav
Adult Children of Emotionally Immature Parents by Lindsay C. Gibson
How to Love by Thich Nhat Hanh

To learn more about mediumship or book a session with Danielle, visit **DanielleHopeWolfe.com**.

acknowledgments

I'd like to take a moment to thank the academy ... Ha! Kidding! But what girl hasn't longed to thank the academy?

In all seriousness, how can I express such immense gratitude to all who have impacted my life, right up until the publication of this book? I have a plethora of individuals that I'd like to acknowledge, so if I neglect to mention your name, please don't be offended—undoubtedly, I remembered my omission just after we went to print, and I'm already planning to make it up to you with home-baked cookies.

Jason: soulmate, best friend, partner. Words can't reflect my feelings for you. In the moment that we met, I knew you were special. I knew that my life would never be the same, but I hadn't the slightest idea how much happiness was in store for us. You are my knight in shining armor. I must have done something amazing in my past life to score you as my husband in this one. No other explanation makes any sense. Thank you for teaching me that love doesn't need to hurt. Thank you for supporting and loving me, especially when I didn't have the slightest clue how to love myself. Thank you for the years of commitment, undying love, forgiveness and unwavering support. You are the beacon of light illuminating my path. I love you and I'm yours forever!

Austin, Kole, Cooper, and Jackson: you are the reasons that I strive to become a better person; you are the energy I look forward to every day. You are my world, and I love you more than words can convey. Thank you for being my biggest teachers in life. You are brilliant, beautiful, amazing souls. I am blessed to be your mama. Thank you for choosing me. I hope for a lifetime of big smiles, summer swimming, watching you grow, and loving you to pieces. My biggest wish is for you: seek happiness and joy around every corner, and never forget how much we love you!

My parents: a beautiful friend recently told me that our mothers are our first loves. I believe this is true, and fathers must be right up there, too. Mom and Dad, you are both my first loves! Human emotions complicate things sometimes— words are uttered that cannot be taken back; feelings are hurt and hearts break—but I remember the bright times more than the dark times. I remember us singing at the top of our lungs on long road trips. I remember hugs, Dr. Who, Hulk Hogan and André the Giant on Sunday mornings. I remember camping trips, roaring laughs, dirt-bike riding and volunteering. I remember you tirelessly driving me to every sports practice and weekend tournament all summer long, and I remember your love. Thank you for doing your best; without you, I wouldn't be where I am today. I love you.

Gram: the woman who has endured more than anyone

I know and always thrives in the face of adversity—you personify the act of making life's lemons into lemonade. Thank you for loving, caring and listening to me. Thanks for your unconditional support, no matter what my decisions. Thanks for having my back and believing that I would achieve whatever I set my mind to accomplishing. Your generous and guiding words are with me forever. I hope that I've made you proud.

Auntie Dale and Aunt Julie: thank you for teaching me grace, humility and love. Thank you for loving me as your own, so fiercely that nothing could prevent your presence in my life. Despite the obstacles of distance, time, schedule or just plain life, you always took time to let me know that I was loved and connected with a beautiful line of people. I love you!

Nicole, Mike and Linda: I am beyond grateful for all of you! Thank you for seeing me, the "baby" of the family, through the worst and best of times. Thank you for the grown-up advice, hugs, love, support and smack on the rear whenever necessary! Thank you for teaching me to toughen up, get dirty, take a punch, and get back up. You are cherished, and I can't imagine life without you. Although we've been through the worst of life's challenges, they always bring us closer. Thank you for being the best older siblings that a girl could ask for in life.

Lauren: a woman who deserves a standing ovation! I am so blessed and thankful to have you in my life! If not for your support, encouragement, beta reading, advice and pep talks, this book would have stopped at Lesson #2. You believed in my book before I believed in my own story. There were several moments when you refused to let me quit and walk away, so thank you. I love you!

Audrey, April, Cathy, Court, Jenna, Lauren, Shelby and the rest of my soul family: Thank you for sitting at my table in life! Thank you for inspiring me to become a better human, friend, companion and soul. I love our late-night chats, early-morning coffee conversations, laughing, crying, growing, kicking ass at life, being your biggest fan, having you as my biggest fans, loving one another through loss, love, divorce, teenagers (no offense kids, someday you will realize that being a parent isn't always easy), successes, graduations, marriages, moves and reunions. We surround ourselves with those we wish to emulate, and I cannot imagine a more inspirational group of women. I love you! I am a better person because of your magic, and the world is a better place because you are here.

Lori, editor turned soul sister: when imagining this book, I prayed for the right people to be placed along my path. You are an answered prayer! I am not quite sure how I got so incredibly blessed to have you in my corner, but I know that you're the "jackpot" in more ways than just editor! In the few months that we've known one another, you've taught me so much about grace, dignity, tact and writing (to name just a few things). I can say with all certainty that you're one of the most intelligent, talented and wise souls I have yet encountered in this life. I am convinced that you're an angel walking among us humans. I hope our friendship continues far beyond the completion of this project.

Megan, I have loved every minute of getting to know you. You are a brilliant teacher and human being, changing so many lives for the better! You live with such beautiful and inspiring purpose. You have taught me invaluable lessons about courage, confidence and self-belief, simply through your interactions, kindness and vulnerability. Thank you so much for your beautiful work, guidance and support in making this story into the best book possible. Along with your awesome team (not to forget the stupendously talented Kelsey, Jazmin, Ira, and those who I haven't even met at the time of writing), you've made my first book-writing and publishing experience a beautiful one! I am 100 percent certain that you are each divinely placed gifts in my life. I feel honored that your hands, minds, and hearts are infused into these pages.

Jazmin Welch at Fleck Creative did a beautiful job elevating my idea of a simple wedding invitation into a gorgeous theme: warm, inviting and soft, with a touch of elegance.

Ex-husbands one, two and three: I couldn't possibly get through the acknowledgments without thanking you for your role in this story, even though I'm fairly certain that you'll never read the book. Without you, I wouldn't have had much to write about. Thank you for contributing to my growth and evolution as a person. We are each the villain in somebody else's story; in some cases, I am the villain in yours. However, you taught me some valuable life lessons, for which I am deeply grateful. Without them, I may not have grown into the person that I am today. I apologize for the ugly and hurtful times, and I wish you lives full of happiness and fulfillment.

Made in the USA
San Bernardino, CA
23 February 2020